EMPOWERING
LEARNERS

Guidelines for School Library Programs

Related Publications:

Standards for the 21st-Century Learner
Available for download from the AASL Web site.
Packets of full-color brochures may be purchased.
Visit www.ala.org/aasl/standards.

Learning4Life (L4L): A National Plan for Implementation of
Standards for the 21st-Century Learner and *Empowering Learners:*
Guidelines for School Library Programs
Available for download at www.ala.org/aasl/learning4life.

Standards for the 21st-Century Learner in Action
Available for purchase at www.alastore.ala.org/aasl.

A Planning Guide for Empowering Learners: with
School Library Program Assessment Rubric
Visit www.ala.org/aasl/planningguide.

The paper used in this publication meets the minimum requirements of
American National Standards for Information Sciences—Permanence of
Paper for Printed Library Materials, ANSI 239.48-1992.

ISBN-13: 978-0-8389-8519-9

Published by:
American Association of School Librarians
a division of the American Library Association
50 E. Huron St.
Chicago, Illinois 60611-2795
To order, call 800-545-2433, press 7
<www.alastore.ala.org/aasl>

Graphic designed by Louis Henry Mitchell.

TABLE OF CONTENTS

PREFACE

As we approach the second decade of the twenty-first century, school library programs continue to undergo momentous changes that have heightened the importance of technology and evidence-based learning. The focus has moved from the library as a confined place to one with fluid boundaries that is layered by diverse needs and influenced by an interactive global community. Guiding principles for school library programs must focus on building a flexible learning environment with the goal of producing successful learners skilled in multiple literacies.

Defining the future direction of school library programs is the purpose of the newest set of guidelines from the American Association of School Librarians (AASL), entitled *Empowering Learners: Guidelines for School Library Programs*. *Empowering Learners* is grounded in the mission of the school library program found in the "Developing Visions for Learning" chapter. The guidelines are supported by the belief that the school librarian "empowers students to be critical thinkers, enthusiastic readers, skillful researchers, and ethical users of information." Evident within the guidelines is a school library program that builds on the constructivist learning theory deep-rooted in the AASL *Standards for the 21st-Century Learner* and supported by the *Standards for the 21st-Century Learner in Action*. The AASL *Standards for the 21st-Century Learner* are presented in a separate publication available for distribution to administrators, teachers, parents, and other community members.

Empowering Learners

Empowering Learners advances school library programs to meet the needs of the changing school library environment and is guided by the *Standards for the 21st-Century Learner* and *Standards for the 21st-Century Learner in Action*. It builds on a strong history of guidelines published to ensure that school library program planners go beyond the basics to provide goals, priorities, criteria, and general principles for establishing effective library programs. A history of guidelines publications for school library programs appears in the appendices of this document.

In December 2006 participants in an AASL Vision Summit, informed by online surveys, began to identify challenges and opportunities that the 21st-century learning environment triggered for school library program administration. Representatives from each state were brought together to help develop a future outlook for the school library profession. The concepts and beliefs generated by the Vision Summit participants provided background for rewriting the school library program guidelines. An AASL Guidelines Editing Task Force was charged with the responsibility for using the information produced at the Vision Summit to develop guidelines for a 21st-century school library program.

As the twenty-first century began, demand that learners master multiple literacies to be successful required new learning standards to address the 21st-century student's instructional styles and needs. The new standards released in October 2007 were published as the *Standards for the 21st-Century Learner*. These new learning standards shift instruction from the narrow focus of information literacy toward a more global direction.

The *Standards for the 21st-Century Learner* require that instruction focuses on the learning process. Because the skills, dispositions, responsibilities, and self-assessment strategies are most effectively taught through integration into diverse content curriculum areas, the AASL Learning Standards Indicators & Assessment Task Force was charged with developing indicators, benchmarks, models, and assessments to expand and support the *Standards for the 21st-Century Learner*. The work of the task force, *Standards for the 21st-Century Learner in Action*, was released by AASL in January 2009. The *Standards for the 21st-Century Learner in Action* is an essential influence on the school library program guidelines in *Empowering Learners*. It provides support in teaching the essential skills defined in the *Standards for the 21st-Century Learner* and confirms that the school library program learning environment must change to support 21st-century student learning.

In the fall of 2008 the AASL Standards and Guidelines Implementation Task Force launched a national plan to implement the learning standards and program guidelines under the brand *Learning4Life (L4L)*. The plan identifies target audiences and training opportunities, and provides a communication plan, as well as a plan for continuous feedback, evaluation, and sustainability. *L4L* includes an endorsement strategy and additional supporting documents. An essential component of this plan is to assist school librarians to recognize and connect the new learning standards and guidelines to content area curriculum standards, resulting in improved teaching and learning.

Empowering Learners envisions the school library program of the future. Its foundation is our mission to ensure that students and staff are effective users of information and ideas, and it is based on the principles expressed in the AASL *Standards for the 21st-Century Learner* and the *Standards for the 21st-Century Learner in Action*. Together these documents, promoted through the *Learning4Life (L4L)* brand, emphasize that school library programs contribute to both school-based learning and learning throughout a lifetime. These current guidelines reflect AASL's professional dedication to provide you with updated standards for your school library program so that you can continue to provide learners with context for instruction and empower lifelong learning.

Ann M. Martin, AASL President, 2008–2009
March 6, 2009

DEVELOPING VISIONS FOR LEARNING

"The school librarian has the opportunity to be the essential member of the instructional team in each school. This responsibility brings an ongoing commitment to the changing curriculum in K–12, innovative teaching, being knowledgeable about how students learn and achieve, and embracing and understanding the dynamic role that the integration of technology contributes to student learning."

– AASL phone interview respondent

I. THE MISSION OF THE SCHOOL LIBRARY PROGRAM

Throughout the history of the school library profession, the essential goals of the school library program have remain unchanged. school librarians strive to instill a love of learning in all students and ensure equitable access to information. However, technologies developed within the past two decades have revolutionized the way we access and use information. The early effects of these changes on the school library program are explored in *Information Power: Building Partnerships for Learning* (AASL and AECT 1998).

The development of social technology tools has created an interconnected global society where learning, social, and work environments have moved across physical boundaries. Today, for example, a student in England can communicate with peers in China through a blog or video stream; a highly skilled professional in India can work virtually for a company based in the United States. To successfully navigate through these fluid boundaries, learners must embody characteristics of global citizenship and be skilled users of information technologies.

By the end of the 20th century society had shifted from the Industrial Age, which centered around jobs in manufacturing, to the Information Age, in which jobs require innovative thinking and problem-solving skills, effective communication skills, teamwork, and the ability to manage information effectively (Partnership for

21st Century Skills 2008). As a result, the aptitudes learners need to be successful in work and in life have evolved to include high-level thinking skills, innovation skills, and collaborative teamwork. As we gain firm footing in the emerging Knowledge Age, jobs that require these skills continue to grow in numbers and are migrating to the countries where workers have these skills (National Governors Association 2008).

In 2009 AASL revised the mission of the school library program to reflect the expanding responsibilities of the school librarian in helping learners develop the skills needed to be successful in work and in life in the twenty-first century. The revised mission statement appears below:

The mission of the school library program is to ensure that students and staff are effective users of ideas and information. The school librarian empowers students to be critical thinkers, enthusiastic readers, skillful researchers, and ethical users of information by:

- collaborating with educators and students to design and teach engaging learning experiences that meet individual needs

- instructing students and assisting educators in using, evaluating, and producing information and ideas through active use of a broad range of appropriate tools, resources, and information technologies

- providing access to materials in all formats, including up-to-date, high-quality, varied literature to develop and strengthen a love of reading

- providing students and staff with instruction and resources that reflect current information needs and anticipate changes in technology and education

- providing leadership in the total education program and advocating for strong school library programs as essential to meeting local, state, and national education goals

The remainder of this chapter describes the elements of the 21st-century learning environment, including a definition of 21st-century skills, characteristics of today's learning environment and its learners, a description of the *Standards for the 21st-Century Learner*, and an exploration of how the roles of the school librarian must expand to advance student learning in this new environment.

II. 21ST-CENTURY SKILLS

In 2002 policymakers and leaders in business and education formed the Partnership for 21st Century Skills, which presently includes such organizations as Apple, Dell, Microsoft Corporation, Intel Corporation, Sesame Workshop, National Education Association, Adobe Systems Incorporated, Education Networks of America, and American Association of School Librarians (AASL), among others. Together, members of the Partnership have identified the competencies learners need to succeed in work and in life in today's environment. The Partnership describes student outcomes that promote a higher level of thinking. These include core subjects and 21st-century themes, learning and innovation skills; information, media, and technology skills; and life and career skills.

DELVE DEEPER

Collins, H. T., F. R. Czarra, and A. F. Smith. 2003. Guidelines for global and international studies education: Challenges, culture, connections. <www. globaled.org/guidelines> (accessed December 11, 2008).

Friedman, T. 2007. *The World Is Flat 3.0: A Brief History of the Twenty-First Century.* New York: Picador.

Li, C. and J. Bernoff. 2008. *Groundswell: Winning in a World Transformed by Social Technologies.* Cambridge, MA: Harvard Business Press.

Partnership for 21st Century Learning. *The Intellectual and Policy Foundations of the 21st Century Skills Framework.* <www.21stcenturyskills. org/route21/images/stories/epapers/ skills_foundations_final.pdf> (accessed January 14, 2009).

Pink, D. 2005. *A Whole New Mind: Moving from the Information Age to the Conceptual Age.* New York: Riverhead Books.

Tapscott, D. and A. D. Williams. 2008. *Wikinomics: How Mass Collaboration Changes Everything,* expanded ed. New York: Portfolio.

TOPIC	DESCRIPTION
Core Subjects	English, reading or language arts; world languages; arts; mathematics; economics; science; geography; history; government and civics
21st-century themes	Global awareness; financial, economic, business, and entrepreneurial literacy; civic literacy; health literacy
Learning and innovation skills	Creativity and innovation skills; critical thinking and problem-solving skills; communication and collaboration skills
Information, media, and technology skills	Information literacy; media literacy; ICT literacy
Life and career skills	Flexibility and adaptability; initiative and self-direction; social and cross-cultural skills; productivity and accountability; leadership and responsibility

Source: The Partnership for 21st Century Skills

The teaching of core subjects is interwoven with 21st-century interdisciplinary themes; learning and innovation skills; life and career skills; and information, media, and technology skills. These key outcomes are supported by the learning standards, assessments, curriculum and instruction, professional development, and the learning environment itself.

DELVE DEEPER

Jenkins, H., et.al. *Confronting the Challenge of Participatory Culture: Media Education for the 21st Century.* Chicago: MacArthur Foundation. http://digitallearning.macfound. org/atf/cf/%7B7E45C7E0-A3E0-4B89-AC9C-E807E1B0AE4E%7D/ JENKINS_WHITE_PAPER.PDF (accessed January 14, 2009).

Mardis, M.A., and A. M. Perrault. 2008. A whole new library: Six "senses" you can use to make sense of new standards and guidelines. *Teacher Librarian* 35, no.4, 34–38.

Wiggins, G, and J. McTighe. 2008. *Schooling by Design: Mission, Action, and Achievement.* Alexandria, VA: ASCD.

III. THE 21ST-CENTURY LEARNING ENVIRONMENT

In a participatory culture where every individual has a voice to contribute, the school librarian, classroom teachers, and students now share the roles of teacher and learner. As a guide, risk-taker, expert at learning how to learn, partner in meeting instructional goals and curriculum development, and information specialist, the school librarian must work to create an environment where everyone is a teacher, learner, producer, and contributor. Patrons of the school library are now collaborators who interact with resources and with each other. Technology is woven throughout this framework, influencing every aspect of teaching and learning.

Digital technologies have created endless opportunities for innovative teaching and learning. Though face-to-face collaboration remains an essential component of learning, virtual tools are now used to connect learning to the world outside the classroom. Educators can bring topics to life through web-based assignments that incorporate a multitude of online resources, including subject-related photographs, video, and audio. Using emerging technologies the school librarian and classroom teacher can create online discussion groups for students to debate a classroom topic. School librarians and classroom teachers can also use such technologies to connect with other educators and experts to seek advice or ideas for class assignments, or to partner with local businesses, educational institutions, and other organizations to blend learning with real-world experiences.

Within the past decade, educational scholars have worked to define the elements that should comprise today's learning environment. As described by the Partnership for 21st Century Skills, learning environments should no longer be thought of as physical spaces, but as the systems that allow learning to take place.

"Perhaps a better way to think of 21st century learning environments is as the support systems that organize the condition in which humans learn best—systems that accommodate the unique learning needs of every learner and support the positive human relationships needed for effective learning. Learning environments are the structures, tools, and communities that inspire students and educators to attain the knowledge and skills the 21st century demands of us all." (Partnership for 21st Century Skills 2009)

For such rich learning environments to flourish, the school librarian must collaborate with administrators, classroom teachers, students, and other members of the learning community to develop the policies that guide the school. Every component of the school—from the physical space to scheduling—should be designed to accommodate a variety of learning styles, from collaborative group work to individual study.

IV. THE 21ST-CENTURY LEARNER

Members of the school library profession may remember a time when computers, e-mail, and the Internet did not exist. However, today's learners have grown up in a "wired" world. They have constant access to global information resources through computers and mobile devices, and they expect to be able to retrieve information instantly. This bold new generation questions the concept of cognitive authority as mob indexing and Wikipedia permeate the Web. Learners are now surrounded by information, whether in print, online, or in sound bites of data.

93% of American teens use the Internet

64% of online teens have participated in content-creating activities on the Internet

28% of online teens have created their own online journal or blog

55% of online teens have created a profile on a social networking site

26% of online teens remix content they find online

Source: Lenhart et al. 2007

Many online learners are content creators who manipulate, remix, and share content, and expect to engage in conversation with other creators. They challenge traditional ideas about intellectual property and fair use, but may lack an understanding of how to use information from the Web ethically.

While a significant number of learners are tech-savvy, a deep digital divide remains between learners with 24–7 access to the Web at home and at school, and those with limited access. By the end of 2005, 24 percent of rural Americans had high-speed Internet access at home, compared with 39 percent of urban and suburban Americans (Horrigan and Murray 2006). Learners with limited Internet access suffer a disadvantage compared to those who grow up with readily available access.

The school librarian works to bridge this digital divide and ensure that all learners are skilled users of information in all formats. Expanded access to computers should be coupled with educational initiatives that help learners become effective users of digital technologies (Jenkins 2006).

V. *STANDARDS FOR THE 21ST-CENTURY LEARNER*

Learning in the twenty-first century has taken on new dimensions with the exponential expansion of information, ever-changing tools, increased digitization of text, and heightened demands for critical and creative thinking, communication, and collaborative problem solving. To succeed in our rapid-paced, global society, learners must develop high-level thinking skills, attitudes, and responsibilities. All learners must be able to access quality information from diverse perspectives, make sense of it to draw their own conclusions or create new knowledge, and share their knowledge with others.

In recognition of these demands, the American Association of School Librarians (AASL) developed standards for the literacy, technology, critical thinking, and information skills that all learners need to acquire. The new standards, entitled *Stan-*

DELVE DEEPER

Kelly, F. S., T. McCain, and I. Jukes. 2008. *Teaching the Digital Generation: No More Cookie-Cutter High Schools.* Thousand Oaks, CA: Corwin.

The Learning Compact Redefined: A Call to Action. A Report of the Commission of the Whole Child. <www.ascd.org/learningcompact> (accessed January 9, 2008).

Lohnes, S. 2007. Situating the Net Gen: Exploring the Role of Technology in the Social Identity of College Students. Paper presented at American Educational Research Association, Chicago, IL, April.

Small, G., and G. Vargan. 2008. *iBrain: Surviving the Technological Alteration of the Modern Mind.* New York: Collins Living.

Wilber, D. 2007. Mynetwork: Understanding the Links and Texts of College Students' New Literacies. Paper presented at American Educational Research Association, Chicago, IL, April.

dards for the 21st-Century Learner, take a fresh approach and a broad perspective on student standards in the school library field by focusing on the learning process, not on the more limited concept of information literacy. They lay out underlying common beliefs, as well as standards and indicators for essential skills, dispositions, responsibilities, and self-assessment strategies for all learners.

The nine common beliefs feature two core approaches to learning that are embedded in school library programs—reading and inquiry. Students who can (and do) read and inquire with thoughtfulness and curiosity are empowered to push their own learning to deeper levels and wider vistas.

Common Beliefs

1. Reading is a window to the world.

Reading is a foundational skill for learning, personal growth, and enjoyment. The degree to which students can read and understand information in all formats (for example, picture, video, print) and all contexts is a key indicator of success in school and in life. As a lifelong learning skill, reading goes beyond decoding and comprehension to interpretation and development of new understandings.

2. Inquiry provides a framework for learning.

To become independent learners, students must gain not only the skills but also the disposition to use those skills, along with an understanding of their own responsibilities and self-assessment strategies. Combined, these four elements build a learner who can thrive in a complex information environment.

3. Ethical behavior in the use of information must be taught.

In this increasingly global world of information, students must be taught to seek diverse perspectives, gather and use information ethically, and use social tools responsibly and safely.

4. Technology skills are crucial for future employment needs.

Today's students need to develop information skills that will enable them to use technology as an important tool for learning, both now and in the future.

5. Equitable access is a key component for education.

All children deserve equitable access to books and reading, to information, and to information technology in an environment that is safe and conducive to learning.

6. The definition of information literacy has become more complex as resources and technologies have changed.

Information literacy has progressed from the simple definition of using printed reference sources to find information. Multiple literacies, including digital, visual, textual, and technological, have now joined information literacy as crucial skills for this century.

7. **The continuing expansion of information demands that all individuals acquire the thinking skills that will enable them to learn on their own.**

   The amount of information available to our learners necessitates that each individual acquire the skills to select, evaluate, and use information appropriately and effectively.

8. **Learning has a social context.**

   Learning is enhanced by opportunities to share and learn with others. Students need to develop skills in sharing knowledge and learning with others, both in face-to-face situations and through technology.

9. **School libraries are essential to the development of learning skills.**

   School libraries provide equitable physical and intellectual access to the resources and tools required for learning in a warm, stimulating, and safe environment. School librarians collaborate with others to provide instruction, learning strategies, and practice in using the essential learning skills needed in the twenty-first century.

Implicit within the nine common beliefs is recognition of the importance of skills that lead to productive behavior. Information literacy, the use of technology, critical thinking, and ethical decision making all have a basis in skills and an actualization in the behaviors that students choose to exhibit—from seeking diverse perspectives, to evaluating information, to using technology appropriately, to applying information literacy skills, to using multiple formats. The common beliefs outline the responsibilities that school librarians and other educators accept for providing environments that support and foster successful learning.

Summary of Learning Standards

The common beliefs describe the learning environment for the new learning standards, which are summarized below. The full text of the standards is available for download at AASL's website <www.aasl.org>.

1. **Inquire, think critically, and gain knowledge.**

   Standard 1 addresses the process of investigating and gaining knowledge. Learners use an inquiry-based process to seek knowledge in curricular subjects and connect this information to the outside world. They demonstrate the ability to critically evaluate information and sources, and to use information presented in a variety of formats. To find information, learners must develop a mastery of technology tools and collaborate with others to learn deeply.

2. Draw conclusions, make informed decisions, apply knowledge to new situations, and create new knowledge.

In Standard 2 learners are expected to extend their knowledge by drawing their own conclusions, making decisions, applying the knowledge to new situations, and creating new knowledge. Learners continue the inquiry-based research process by applying critical-thinking skills to information and knowledge to create and organize new knowledge. They use a mastery of technology and other information tools to analyze and organize information, and collaborate with others to exchange ideas, develop new understandings, make decisions, and solve problems. Furthermore, learners use writing, media, and visual literacy skills, and technology skills to create products that express new understandings.

3. Share knowledge and participate ethically and productively as members of our democratic society.

In today's interconnected world, learners must go beyond the knowledge they have gained independently because they are increasingly called upon to collaborate and share their knowledge with others, while following ethical guidelines. Learners conclude the inquiry-based research process using technology and other information tools to organize and display new knowledge and understandings. They are able to connect learning to community issues, and use information and technology ethically and responsibly.

4. Pursue personal and aesthetic growth.

At the apex of the learning taxonomy is the pursuit of personal and aesthetic growth—the motivation and skills to learn on one's own to satisfy internal needs and interests. Learners read, view, and listen for pleasure and seek information for personal learning. They are able to connect ideas to their own interests and previous knowledge, organize personal knowledge, use social networks and information tools to gather and share information, and express personal learning through creative and artistic methods.

Strands of Learning

Four strands of learning are delineated in *Standards for the 21st-Century Learner*: skills, dispositions in action, responsibilities, and self-assessment strategies. Any learning is based on skills; in fact, national standards in every curriculum area outline some of the skills, as well as the content, for that discipline. These AASL learning standards, however, take a broader approach to the learning process. Successful learners have developed not only the skills of learning, but also the dispositions to use the skills.

Dispositions are the learning behaviors, attitudes, and habits of mind that transform a learner from one who is able to learn to one who actually does learn. Dispositions can be taught by structuring assignments and learning environments so that they require persistence, flexibility, divergent thinking, or any other learning behavior. Dispositions can be assessed through documentation that proves the learner has followed the behavior during the learning process. For example, the student may be asked to document a critical stance with two-column notes: the left column containing information and the right column containing the student's evaluation of this information.

Responsibilities make up the third strand included in the standards. The goal of any educational system is to enable students to emerge as responsible and productive members of society. For that to happen, students must be taught responsibility over the years of schooling. Probably the most effective method of teaching responsibility is to follow a process of gradual release of responsibility, in which the teacher assumes a strong, guiding role at first and then gradually transfers that responsibility to the student as he or she develops the capacity to assume it. For example, students who are expected to respect copyright and intellectual property rights must learn through a series of experiences how to avoid plagiarism and to rely on their own thinking.

In recognition of the importance of self-regulation in any learning process, the fourth strand contains self-assessment strategies. Learners must be able to look at their own work to determine its quality, discover gaps in their own thinking, ask questions to lead to further investigation, find areas that need revision or rethinking, recognize their new understandings, and determine when they need to ask for help. The metacognitive aspects of self-assessment lead to higher levels of thinking and self-monitoring. Self-assessment complements, but does not replace, assessment by the school librarian and classroom teacher.

A full discussion of the learning standards as well as action examples and benchmarks can be found in *Standards for the 21st-Century Learner in Action* (SIA). SIA includes indicators, benchmarks, model examples, and assessments to support school librarians and other educators in teaching the essential learning skills defined in the learning standards. It also presents action examples for putting the standards into practice in elementary, middle, and high school classrooms.

VI. THE CHANGING ROLES OF THE SCHOOL LIBRARIAN

In December 2006 the AASL Board of Directors organized an assembly to create the envisioned future of the profession within a 21st-century learning environment. The Vision Summit brought together leading school librarians from all parts of the country; they represented diverse backgrounds and experiences. Prior to the Vision Summit, AASL conducted telephone interviews and Web surveys with members of the educational community to inform the discussion.

DELVE DEEPER

American Association of School Librarians. 2007. *Standards for the 21st-century learner.*<www.ala.org/aasl/standards> (accessed February 23, 2009).

American Association of School Librarians. 2009. *Standards for the 21st-century learner in action.* Chicago: ALA.

Coatney, S. 2008. Standards for the 21st-century learner. *school library Media Activities Monthly* 24, no.6, 56–58.

Dickinson, G. K. 2008. A place to stand. *Library Media Connection* 26, no.6, 10–12.

Donham, J. 2008. Standards! Standards! Standards! *Teacher Librarian* 35, no.4, 43–46.

Johns, S. K. 2008. AASL standards for the 21st-century learner: A time to reflect and study. *CSLA Journal* 31, no.2, 8–9.

Midland, S. 2008. From stereopticon to Google: Technology and school library standards. *Teacher Librarian* 35, no.4, 30–33.

DELVE DEEPER

LEADER

Carr, J., ed. (for AASL). 2008. *Leadership for Excellence: Insights of the National school library Media Program of the Year Award winners.* Chicago: ALA Editions.

Fullan, M. 2008. *The Six Secrets of Change: What the Best Leaders Do to Help Their Organizations Survive and Thrive.* Hoboken, NJ: Jossey Bass.

Hord, S. M. and W. A. Sommers. 2008. *Leading Professional Learning Communities: Voices From Research and Practice.* Thousand Oaks, CA: Corwin.

Lance, K. and D. V. Loertscher. 2005. *Powering Achievement,* 3rd ed. Salt Lake City: Hi Willow Research and Publishing.

Perrault, A. M. 2007. Schools as information ecologies: A proposed framework of study. *School Libraries Worldwide* 13, no.2, 49–62.

A selected group of school librarians and administrators participated in telephone interviews in which they were asked to identify key features that school library programs need to meet the challenges and opportunities facing education. Survey participants identified several trends in the school library program. These included the need to provide open access to library information resources 24–7; to implement projects that involve global networking; to integrate technology directly with curriculum; to connect the school library program outcomes to broader learning outcomes and measurements; and to substantially increase collaboration with classroom teachers, anticipating their needs and driving information to them.

Online survey respondents, which included AASL members and nonmembers, identified the shifting responsibilities of the school librarian. Respondents were asked to rank the four primary roles commonly used today in describing the functions of the school librarian—teacher, instructional partner, information specialist, and program administrator—in order of importance to the respondents' current positions. They were then asked to rank the four primary roles describing the functions of the school librarian in order of importance to the future success of school library programs. The responses (table 1) show a shift toward the roles of instructional partner and information specialist as central to the school library program.

Table 1. School librarians' ranking of their roles now and in the future.

NOW			FUTURE	
ROLE	RANK		ROLE	RANK
Teacher	1		Instructional Partner	1
Information Specialist	2		Information Specialist	2
Instructional Partner	3		Teacher	3
Program Administrator	4		Program Administrator	4

Using this research as a backdrop, Vision Summit participants brainstormed current roles of the school librarian to explore how they must change to bring the school library program into the twenty-first century. In addition to the four key roles named in the phone and Web survey, Vision Summit participants identified "leader" as an additional role that is essential to the future of the profession. In exploring these five roles, several themes emerged. Among them was the need to increase accountability in connection with student performance, to broaden the reach of the school library program to a global level, to model emerging technologies to reach learners, and to create virtual 24–7 access to the school library.

Leader

Leadership is integral to developing a successful 21st-century school library program. As information literacy and technology skills become central to learning, the school librarian must lead the way in building 21st-century skills throughout the school environment. Doing so involves a willingness to serve as a teacher and a learner who listens to and acts upon good ideas from peers, teachers, and students. Leadership also requires increased professional commitment and thorough knowledge of the challenges and opportunities facing the profession. By becoming an active member of the local and global learning community, the school librarian can build relationships with organizations and stakeholders to develop an effective school library program and advocate for student learning.

Instructional Partner

As outlined in *Information Power: Building Partnerships for Learning*, the school librarian works with members of the school community to develop the policies, practices, and curricula to guide student learning. The school librarian collaborates with classroom teachers to develop assignments that are matched to academic standards and include key critical thinking skills, technology and information literacy skills, and core social skills and cultural competencies. The school librarian guides instructional design by working with the classroom teacher to establish learning objectives and goals, and by implementing assessment strategies before, during, and after assigned units of study. In a 24–7 learning environment, communication with classroom teachers and students now takes place virtually, as well as face-to-face.

Information Specialist

AASL survey respondents and Vision Summit participants both identified the crucial role that technology plays in every aspect of the school library program. As an information specialist the school librarian uses technology tools to supplement school resources, assist in the creation of engaging learning tasks, connect the school with the global learning community, communicate with students and classroom teachers at any time, and provide 24–7 access to library services. The school librarian introduces and models emerging technologies, as well as strategies for finding, assessing, and using information. He or she is a leader in software and hardware evaluation, establishing the processes for such evaluation to take place. Doing so requires frequent evaluation of the use of technology in the school library through regular data analysis.

Expertise in the ethical use of information also remains a cornerstone of the school librarian's role as information specialist. As copyright options continue to expand for creators, the school librarian must be versed in the theoretical grounding and practical application of such laws in order to teach the ethical use of information to the learning community. This involves new understandings of fair use and forms of licensing that allow users to modify original content. Students, teachers, and other members of the educational community look to the school librarian to set guidelines for navigating fair use issues.

INSTRUCTIONAL PARTNER

Gregory, G. H. and L. Kuzmich. 2007. *Teacher Teams That Get Results: 61 Strategies for Sustaining and Renewing Professional Learning Communities.* Thousand Oaks, CA: Corwin.

Villa, R. A., J. S. Thousand, and A. I. Nevin. 2008. *A Guide to Co-Teaching: Practical Tips for Facilitating Student Learning.* Thousand Oaks, CA: Corwin.

Wiggins, G., and J. McTighe. 2005. *Understanding by Design*, expanded 2nd ed. Alexandria, VA: ASCD.

Wild, M. D., A. S. Mayeaux, and K. P. Edmonds. 2008. *TeamWork: Setting the Standard for Collaborative Teaching, Grades 5–9*. Portland, ME: Stenhouse.

Williams, R.B. 2008. *More Than 50 Ways to Build Team Consensus.* Thousand Oaks, CA: Corwin.

INFORMATION SPECIALIST

Children and Electronic Media, 2008. *The Future of Children* 18, no.1 (Spring). <www.futureofchildren. org/usr_doc/Media_Summary.pdf> (accessed January 14, 2009).

Jonassen, D. H., J. Howland, R. M. Marra, and D. P. Crismond. 2007. *Meaningful Learning with Technology*, 3rd ed. New York: Prentice-Hall.

November, A. 2008. *Web Literacy for Educators.* Thousand Oaks, CA: Corwin.

Pitler, H., E. R. Hubbell, M. Kuhn, and K. Malenoski. 2007. *Using Technology with Classroom Instruction That Works.* Alexandria, VA: ASCD.

Rose, D. and A. Meyer. 2002. *Teaching Every Student in the Digital Age.* Alexandria, VA: ASCD.

Warlick, D. 2005. *Raw Materials for the Mind: A Teacher's Guide to Digital Literacy.* Lulu.com. <www.lulu.com/content/116469> (accessed January 14, 2009).

TEACHER

Danielson, C. 2007. *Enhancing Professional Practice: a Framework for Teachers.* 2nd ed. Alexandria, VA: ASCD.

Heppell, S. 2008. *It Simply Isn't the 20th Century Any More Is It?: So Why Would We Teach as Though It Was?* Video lecture. (October 13). http://k12onlineconference.org/?p=268 (accessed January 14, 2009).

Jensen, E. 2008. *Brain-Based Learning: The New Paradigm of Teaching,* 2nd ed. Thousand Oaks, CA: Corwin.

Valli, L. and D. Bueses. 2007. The changing role of teachers in an era of high-stakes accountability. *American Educational Research Journal* 44, no.3, 519–58.

Zuljian, M. V. 2007. Students' conceptions of knowledge, the role of the teacher and learner as important factors in a didactic school reform. *Educational Studies* 33, no.1, 29–40.

PROGRAM ADMINISTRATOR

Fichtman, N. D. and D. Yendol-Hoppey. 2008. *The Reflective Educator's Guide to Professional Development: Coaching Inquiry-Oriented Learning Communities.* Thousand Oaks, CA: Corwin.

Fontichiaro, K. 2008. Planning an online professional development module. *school library Media Activities Monthly* 25, no.2, 30–31.

Kerby, R. N. 2006. *Collection Development for the school library Media Program: A Beginner's Guide.* Chicago: ALA.

Kern, K. 2009. *Virtual Reference Best Practices: Tailoring Services to Your Library.* Chicago: ALA.

Montiel-Overall, P. and D. C. Adcock, editors. 2009. *school library Services in a Multicultural Society.* Chicago: AASL.

Woolls, B. 2008. *The school library Media Manager,* 4th ed. Westport, CT: Libraries Unlimited.

Teacher

As teacher the school librarian empowers students to become critical thinkers, enthusiastic readers, skillful researchers, and ethical users of information. The school librarian supports students' success by guiding them to:

- read for understanding, breadth, and pleasure
- use information for defined and self-defined purposes
- build on prior knowledge and construct new knowledge
- embrace the world of information and all its formats
- work with each other in successful collaborations for learning
- constructively assess their own work and the work of their peers
- become their own best critics.

The school librarian advocates for reading for pleasure and supports reading comprehension skills across all formats. By being conversant with new research about reading, the school librarian can build a collection that reflects the needs of learners from a variety of backgrounds and cultures, and with diverse abilities and aspirations. A leading school librarian stays abreast of both national trends of popular reading material and student interests within the individual school community. He or she advocates for reading in all formats, such as graphic novels, periodicals, and online sources.

Program Administrator

As program administrator, the school librarian ensures that all members of the learning community have access to resources that meet a variety of needs and interests. The implementation of a successful school library program requires the collaborative development of the program mission, strategic plan, and policies, as well as the effective management of staff, the program budget, and the physical and virtual spaces. To augment information resources available to the learning community, the school librarian works actively to form partnerships with stakeholders and sister organizations at local and global levels. The school librarian also addresses broader educational issues with other educators in the building, at the district level, and at the professional association level.

All of these five roles—leader, instructional partner, teacher, information specialist, and program administrator—are interconnected; one cannot be performed without the support of the others. Teaching for learning requires collaboration with classroom teachers and students to design engaging lessons and units of study (as an instructional partner), knowledge of what technologies can support learning (as an information specialist), effective program administration to ensure quality resources are available for learners, and leadership to establish the way forward. The responsibilities of these roles are interwoven throughout the guidelines that follow in the "Teaching for Learning" and "Building the Learning Environment" chapters. Because leadership is the essential element to delivering an effective 21st-century school library program, this role is explored further in the concluding chapter.

TEACHING FOR LEARNING

GUIDELINES

1. The school library program promotes collaboration among members of the learning community and encourages learners to be independent, lifelong users and producers of ideas and information.

2. The school library program promotes reading as a foundational skill for learning, personal growth, and enjoyment.

3. The school library program provides instruction that addresses multiple literacies, including information literacy, media literacy, visual literacy, and technology literacy.

4. The school library program models an inquiry-based approach to learning and the information search process.

5. The school library program is guided by regular assessment of student learning to ensure the program is meeting its goals.

The school librarian serves as a leader in implementing quality instruction and creating authentic learning experiences. As a teacher, instructional partner, and information specialist, the school librarian is uniquely poised to function as an agent of change. The school librarian teaches in what is usually the school building's largest space for learning and knows the resources available to classroom teachers and students. He or she understands the curriculum of the school thoroughly and can partner with teachers to create exciting learning experiences in an information- and media-rich environment. The school librarian is also cognizant of the varied teaching and learning styles of classroom teachers and students. These multiple knowledge bases allow the school librarian to lead from the center, guiding learning to meet the needs of all 21st-century learners.

Learning in the library takes place in a variety of ways, from the formal inquiry process of whole-class instruction, to drop-in review sessions, and to small group and individual learning. Instruction is built on the foundation of constructivism, a theory of active learning in which students guide and continually assess the

DELVE DEEPER

Harada, V., C. H. Kirio, and S. H.
    Yamamoto. *Collaborating for
    Project-Based Learning in Grades
    9–12*. Columbus, OH: Linworth Books.

Mardis, M. A. 2007. Unpacking the
    baggage of collaboration: Some
    factors to consider. *Media Spectrum*
    33, no.3, 10–11.

Mardis, M. A., and E. S. Hoffman. 2007.
    Collection and collaboration:
    Science in Michigan middle school
    media centers. *school library Media
    Research* 10. Chicago: AASL. <www.
    ala.org/ala/mgrps/divs/aasl/aaschool
    library programub-
    sandjournals/slmrb/slmrcontents/
    volume10/mardis_collectionandcol-
    laboration.cfm> (accessed January
    14, 2009).

Montiel-Overall, P., and D. C. Adcock, eds.
    2007. *Collaboration*. Best of KQ 1.
    Chicago: ALA.

learning process. With the school librarian and classroom teacher as their guides, students build on prior knowledge and experiences to construct new knowledge. The school librarian and classroom teacher assist this process, tailoring teaching methods to meet learners' needs. By reflecting on the learning process, students learn *how* to learn while constructing new knowledge.

I. BUILDING COLLABORATIVE PARTNERSHIPS

GUIDELINE: The school library program promotes collaboration among members of the learning community and encourages learners to be independent, lifelong users and producers of ideas and information.

ACTIONS: The school librarian:

– collaborates with a core team of classroom teachers and specialists to design, implement, and evaluate inquiry lessons and units

– collaborates with an extended team that includes parents, members of the community, museums, academic and public libraries, municipal services, private organizations, and commercial entities to include their expertise and assistance in inquiry lessons and units

– works with administrators to actively promote, support, and implement collaboration

– seeks input from students on the learning process

The teaching of 21st-century skills requires that all aspects of teaching and learning are built on collaborative partnerships. As an instructional partner the school librarian assists classroom teachers in developing inquiry-driven curricular units that effectively teach content and research skills to students of all learning styles. As a teacher the school librarian collaborates with students to build information literacy skills and identify appropriate tools for collecting, communicating, finding, and using information. These collaborative partnerships require creativity, an openness to trying new approaches, and a willingness to take risks.

In today's learning environment, the line between teacher and student has blurred. All members of the learning community now share the roles of teacher, learner, and collaborative partner. Together with the classroom teacher, the school librarian empowers students to take an active role in shaping their learning. The school librarian also plays a role as learner, absorbing knowledge from students, classroom teachers, and other educators. For example, the school librarian can learn from students about popular new technologies. In turn, the school librarian can research these technologies and demonstrate how they can be used effectively in the learning environment. By modeling such collaborative relationships, the school librarian helps change the culture of the learning community to reflect the kind of relationships that comprise the 21st-century work environment.

Collaboration also takes place beyond school walls. The school librarian links the school library with the greater school, library, and education community through collaborative programs, cooperative collection development, and interlibrary loans. Partnering with community organizations, such as museums, colleges, universities, local businesses, public and academic libraries, and civic groups, can enrich the program through added resources and interaction with the world outside the school.

DELVE DEEPER

Braunger, J. and J. P. Lewis. 2006. *Building a Knowledge Base in Reading*, 2nd ed. Urbana, IL: NCTE.

Bush, G. 2005. *Every Student Reads: Collaboration and Reading to Learn.* Chicago: ALA.

Fogarty, R. *Literacy Matters*. 2007. 2nd ed. Thousand Oaks, CA: Corwin.

Harvey, S. and A. Goudvis. 2007. *Strategies that Work: Teaching Comprehension for Understanding and Engagement*, 2nd ed. Portland, ME: Stenhouse.

Ivey, G. and D. Fisher. 2006. *Creating Literacy-Rich Schools for Adolescents.* Alexandria, VA: ASCD.

Kajder, S. 2008. The book trailer: Engaging teens through technologies. *Educational Leadership* 65, no.6. <www.ascd.org/publications/educational_leadership/mar08/vol65/num06/The_Book_Trailer@_Engaging_Teens_Through_Technologies.aspx> (accessed January 14, 2009).

Koechlin, C. and S. Zwaan. 2006. *Build Your Own Information Literate School.* Salt Lake City: Hi Willow Research and Publishing.

Krashen, S. 2006. *The Power of Reading*, 2nd ed. Westport, CT: Libraries Unlimited.

Moreillon, J. 2007. *Collaborative Strategies for Teaching Reading Comprehension: Maximizing Your Impact.* Chicago: ALA.

Ohler, J. 2007. *Digital Storytelling in the Classroom: New Media Pathways to Literacy, Learning, and Creativity.* Thousand Oaks, CA: Corwin.

Warlick, D. 2009. *Redefining Literacy 2.0*, 2nd ed. Columbus, OH: Linworth Books.

II. THE ROLE OF READING

GUIDELINE: The school library program promotes reading as a foundational skill for learning, personal growth, and enjoyment.

ACTIONS: The school librarian:

— models reading strategies in formal and informal instruction

— collaborates with teachers and other specialists to integrate reading strategies into lessons and units of instruction

— acquires and promotes current, high-quality, high-interest collections of books and other reading resources in multiple formats

— develops initiatives to encourage and engage learners in reading, writing, and listening for understanding and enjoyment

— fosters reading for various pursuits, including personal pleasure, knowledge, and ideas

— creates an environment where independent reading is valued, promoted, and encouraged

— motivates learners to read fiction and nonfiction through reading aloud, booktalking, displays, exposure to authors, and other means

— creates opportunities to involve caregivers, parents, and other family members in reading

As the first common belief in the *Standards for the 21st-Century Learner* indicates, the promotion of reading for pleasure and learning remains at the core of the school library program. Learners must have opportunities to read for enjoyment, as well as for information.

THE LEARNER IS ABLE TO:

– Build upon prior knowledge to make sense of new information

– Ask questions about the text before, during, and after reading

– Monitor comprehension by summarizing, predicting, and using fix-up strategies

– Determine what is important

– Draw inferences from the text

– Make connections

– Synthesize information to create new knowledge

Reading is a foundational skill for 21st-century learners. Guiding learners to become engaged and effective users of ideas and information, and to appreciate literature, requires that they develop as strategic readers who can comprehend, analyze, and evaluate text in both print and digital formats. The school librarian is in a unique and critical position to partner with other educators to elevate the reading development of learners.

Reading skills involve thinking skills. The extent to which young people use information depends upon their ability to understand what they read, to integrate their understandings with what they already know, and to realize their unanswered questions. To this end, school librarians model and collaboratively teach reading comprehension strategies: assess and use background knowledge, pose and answer questions that are appropriate to the task, make predictions and inferences, determine main ideas, and monitor reading comprehension, as well as the learning process.

In addition, 21st-century learners must become adept at determining authority and accuracy of information, and analyzing and evaluating that information to synthesize new knowledge from multiple resources. School librarians model and collaboratively teach these skills and strategies. Through the development of reading skills, learners are able to begin internalizing information and make connections with what they already know. Learning takes place within this process of construction as learners understand, apply, analyze, and evaluate information, and create new knowledge.

With a deep knowledge of the wide variety of high-quality reading materials available in the library and beyond, the school librarian has a key role in supporting print and online reading comprehension strategy instruction in collaboration with classroom teachers and reading specialists. School librarians co-design, co-implement, and co-evaluate interdisciplinary lessons and units of instruction that result in increased student learning. Such lessons should be designed to promote strategic reading, where students use prior knowledge to actively construct and interpret meaning from text.

While the responsibility for the successful implementation of reading promotion and instruction is shared by the entire school community, the school library serves as a hub of literacy learning in the school. School librarys provide learners, staff, and families with open access to a varied, non-graded, high-quality collection of reading materials in multiple formats to reflect academic needs and personal interests of all members of the learning community. The school librarian partners with classroom teachers, specialists, and other literacy colleagues to make decisions about reading initiatives and reading comprehension instruction, and to develop all learners' curiosity in, and intellectual access to, appropriate resources in all formats and media.

III. ADDRESSING MULTIPLE LITERACIES

GUIDELINE: The school library program provides instruction that addresses multiple literacies, including information literacy, media literacy, visual literacy, and technology literacy.

ACTIONS: The school librarian:

– collaborates with classroom teachers to embed skills associated with multiple literacies into lessons and curricular units

– guides students and teachers to formats most appropriate to the learning task

– promotes critical thinking by connecting learners with the world of information in multiple formats

– provides instruction specific to searching for information in various formats

– stays abreast of emerging technologies and formats

– adapts to and models new skills, new technologies, and new understandings of the learning process

– encourages the use of multiple formats to present data and information in compelling and useful ways

– integrates the use of state-of-the-art and emerging technologies as a means for effective and creative learning

– embeds key concepts of legal, ethical and social responsibilities in accessing, using and creating information in various formats

As resources and technologies continue to change, the teaching of information literacy—the ability to find, comprehend, assess, use, and share information—has grown more complex. The number of information sources and the variety of formats available can leave many information seekers struggling to identify accurate, reliable sources of information. However, the Web and emerging technologies also give the school librarian opportunities to present data and information in compelling and useful ways.

DELVE DEEPER

Association of College and Research Libraries. 2003. Introduction to information literacy. <www.ala.org/ala/mgrps/divs/acrl/issues/infolit/infolitoverview/introtoinfolit/introinfolit.cfm> (accessed December 10, 2008).

Braden, R. A., and J. A. Horton. 1982. Identifying the theoretical foundations of visual literacy. *Journal of Visual/Verbal Languaging* 2, 37–42.

Center for Media Literacy. n.d. Media literacy: A definition …and more. <www.medialit.org/reading_room/rr2def.php> (accessed December 11, 2008).

Gardner, H. 1999. *Intelligence Reframed: Multiple Intelligences for the 21st Century*. New York: Basic Books.

Gilster, P. 1997. *Digital literacy*. New York: Wiley.

International Society for Technology in Education. 2008. "NETS for Teachers 2008." <www.iste.org/Content/NavigationMenu/NETS/ForTeachers/2008Standards/NETS_for_Teachers_2008.htm> (accessed December 29, 2008).

International Society for Technology in Education. 2007. "NETS for Students 2007." <www.iste.org/Content/NavigationMenu/NETS/ForStudents/2007Standards/NETS_for_Students_2007.htm> (accessed January 1, 2008).

State Educational Technology Directors Association, Technology Literacy Assessment Work Group. Technology literacy. <www.nde.state.ne.us/techcen/Technology Literacy.html> (accessed December 11, 2008).

SOME COMMON 21ST-CENTURY LITERACIES

Digital Literacy

The ability to find, use, analyze, and produce information using digital technology

Visual Literacy

The ability to "understand and use images, including the ability to think, learn, and express oneself in terms of images" (Braden and Hortin, 1982, 41)

Textual Literacy

The ability to read, write, analyze, and evaluate textual works of literature, and personal and professional documents

Technological Literacy

The ability to responsibly use appropriate technology to communicate, solve problems, and access, manage, integrate, evaluate, and create information to improve learning in all subject areas and to acquire lifelong knowledge and skills in the 21st century (SETDA)

The use of multimedia technologies and global resources can help create authentic learning experiences that teach 21st-century skills and connect what students are learning to the outside world. Such learning experiences are framed within inquiry-based learning and assessment, where students guide their own learning process with the support of the school librarian and classroom teacher.

Teaching the ethical use of information is paramount in an environment where students regularly produce content that samples or builds upon others' work. As copyright and fair use issues grow more complex, the school librarian must lead the way in navigating this terrain. To do so the school librarian must be well versed in the latest trends regarding fair use, including the expansion of forms of licensing that allow users to reproduce or sample the original content.

IV. EFFECTIVE PRACTICES FOR INQUIRY

GUIDELINE: The school library program models an inquiry-based approach to learning and the information search process.

ACTIONS: The school librarian:

– supports educational and program standards as defined by the local, state, and national associations

– stimulates critical thinking through the use of learning activities that involve application, analysis, evaluation, and creativity

– designs learning tasks that incorporate the information search process

– builds upon learners' prior knowledge as needed for the learning task

– provides aids that help learners collect information and data

– uses differentiated strategies with respect to gender, reading ability, personal interests, and prior knowledge to engage learners in reading and inquiry

– uses diagnostics, including observation, checklists, and graphic organizers, to identify zones of intervention

– applies appropriate interventions to help learners perform tasks that they cannot complete without assistance

– uses formative assessments to guide learners and assess their progress

– provides opportunities for learners to revise their work through feedback from educators and peers

– integrates the use of state-of-the-art and emerging technologies as a means for effective and creative learning

– adapts to and models new technologies and new understandings of the learning process

The school librarian partners with the classroom teacher in the creation, implementation, and assessment of inquiry-driven curricular units that effectively teach multiple literacies as well as content and research skills. Inquiry is a student-centered approach to learning in which students interact with information, use existing knowledge to form new understandings, and use newly formed skills to construct new knowledge. Inquiry shifts the focus of learning from a right or wrong answer to the process of learning and investigation (Kulthau 2007). By learning to formulate appropriate research questions, organize the search for data, analyze and evaluate the data found, and communicate the results, students develop the skills, dispositions, responsibilities, and self-assessment strategies needed to become independent, lifelong learners.

DELVE DEEPER

Blos, S., and J. Krauss. 2007. *Reinventing Project-Based Learning: Your Field Guide to Real-World Projects in the Digital Age.* Washington, DC: ISTE.

Callison, D., and L. Preddy. 2006. *The Blue Book on Information Age Inquiry, Instruction, and Literacy.* Westport, CT: Libraries Unlimited.

Darling-Hammond, L. 2008. *Powerful Learning: What We Know About Teaching for Understanding.* San Francisco, CA: Jossey-Bass.

Gagnon, G. W., and M. Collay. 2006. *Constructivist Learning Design: Key Questions to Teaching to Standards.* Thousand Oaks, CA: Corwin.

Hyerle, D. 2008. *Visual Tools for Transforming Information into Knowledge.* 2nd ed. Thousand Oaks, CA: Corwin.

Koechlin, C., and S. Zwaan. 2006. *Q Tasks: How to Empower Students to Ask Questions and Care About Answers.* Markham, ON: Pembroke Publishers.

Kuhlthau, C. 2004. *Seeking Meaning: A Process Approach to Library and Information Services.* Westport, CT: Libraries Unlimited.

Kuhlthau, C., L. K. Maniotes, and A. K. Caspari. 2007. *Guided Inquiry: Learning in the 21st Century.* Greenwood, CT: Libraries Unlimited.

Loertscher, D. V., C. Koechlin, and S. Zwaan. 2007. *Beyond Bird Units: 18 Models for Teaching and Learning in Information-Rich and Technology-Rich Environments.* Salt Lake City: Hi Willow Research and Publishing.

Loertscher, D. V., and R. Todd. 2007. *We Boost Achievement.* Salt Lake City: Hi Willow Research and Publishing.

Tomlinson, C. A., K. Brimijoin, and L. Narvaez. 2008. *The Differentiated School: Making Revolutionary Changes in Teaching and Learning.* Alexandria, VA: ASCD.

Zmuda, A., and V. H. Harada. 2008. *Librarians as Learning Specialists: Meeting the Learning Imperatives for he 21st Century.* Westport, CT: Libraries Unlimited.

1. The teacher and school librarian collaborate to identify subject goals and objectives to be learned.

2. The teacher and school librarian collaborate to identify the learning standard indicator that will facilitate learning the content.*

3. The teacher and school librarian identify the learning task and formative assessments that will guide the learner.

4. The teacher and school librarian facilitate activities, such as brainstorming and mapping, to help learners articulate their prior knowledge of the topic.

5. The school librarian collaborates with the classroom teacher to use his or her subject goals and objectives as a guide to choosing the information skills for the lesson or unit. The goals and objectives of the learning standards should grow out of the needs of learners in the context of the lesson or unit.

*This should include at least one learning standard indicator that relates to the kinds of questions and methods of inquiry used by the subject area (for example, for history: documentation, citation of primary/secondary sources).

Throughout the inquiry-based task, the school librarian guides learners through the information search process—the steps learners take to find information. There are many models that the school librarian can use to guide learners through the information search process. However, each information search process should ensure that learners are motivated during task initiation by their personal interests or by a skillful presentation of the targeted subject area. Learners' prior knowledge must also be activated in the task initiation and topic selection stages. Additionally, learners must be actively engaged in authentic tasks that are based on real-life roles and/or real-life problems.

The information search process should always include student participation in authentic assessments through self- and peer-assessment, as well as teacher-driven assessments that inform instruction. Instructional interventions are identified by the classroom teacher and school librarian based on observations made during the information search process, ongoing formative assessments, and summative assessments that reflect assessment of the process, as well as the product.

Student feedback should be used to direct the planning, implementation, and assessment of future assignments.

While school curricula often test analytical, mathematical, or linguistic skills, many learners excel in areas outside these traditional fields. Instructional design must address a variety of learning styles, giving every student a chance to find his or her strengths. The school librarian and classroom teacher collaborate in developing challenging and engaging tasks designed to accommodate varied learning styles and address learning difficulties. At the end of a curricular unit, students are free to choose end projects that involve their own skills and interests. These projects may be outside such traditional skill areas as logic, math, and language. A strong library collection that includes a variety of print, audio, and visual resources, and multiple types of workspaces can help support every child's learning style.

V. ASSESSMENT IN TEACHING FOR LEARNING

GUIDELINE: The school library program is guided by regular assessment of student learning to ensure the program is meeting its goals.

ACTIONS: The school librarian:

– uses formative assessments that give students feedback and the chance to revise their work

– uses summative assessments of process and product in collaboration with teachers

– uses performance-based assessments, such as rubrics, checklists, portfolios, journals, observation, conferencing, and self-questioning

– creates rubrics for student work that integrate curricular, informational, and critical thinking standards

– documents student progress through portfolios that demonstrate growth

– implements critical analysis and evaluation strategies

– solicits student input for the assessment of inquiry-based instructional units upon their completion

– solicits student input for post-assessment of inquiry-based instructional units

DELVE DEEPER

Coatney, S. 2003. Assessment for learning. *Curriculum connections through the library*. B. K. Stripling and S. Hughes- Hassell, eds. Westport, CT: Libraries Unlimited, 157–68.

Harada, V. H., and J. M. Yoshina. 2005. *Assessing Learning: Librarians and Teachers as Partners*. Westport, CT: Libraries Unlimited.

Konings, K. D., M. J. van Zundert, S. Brand-Gruwel, and J. J. G. van Merrienboer. 2007. Participatory design in secondary education: Is it a good idea? Students' and teachers' opinions on its desirability and feasibility. *Educational Studies* 33, no.44, 445–67.

Marzano, R. J., and J. S. Kendall. 2008. *Designing and Assessing Educational Objectives: Applying the New Taxonomy*. Thousand Oaks, CA: Corwin.

Pike, M. A. 2007. Values and visibility: The implementation and assessment of citizenship education in schools. *Educational Review* 59, no.2, 215–30.

Popham, J. W. *Transformative Assessment*. 2008. Alexandria, VA: ASCD.

Vance, A. L., and R. Nickle, eds. 2007. *Assessing Student Learning in the school library*. Chicago: AASL.

To meet the needs of learners today, schools must evolve from a 20th-century industrial model to a dynamic, fluid environment that promotes high-order thinking. Teaching should follow this model by continually changing to meet learners' needs. The school librarian and other educators perform regular assessment of the learning process to gather information that will guide teaching and learning.

Throughout each unit of study, the school librarian and classroom teacher collect data on students' processes of seeking, evaluating, and using information to create a final product. Assessment is performed:

– by the student through self-assessments

– by the student working with the classroom teacher and/or school librarian to assess the student's progress during a unit of study

– by the classroom teacher and school librarian to improve instruction during the unit of study

– by the school librarian to determine how well the program is working to improve student achievement.

TYPES OF FORMATIVE ASSESSMENTS

- Checklists
- Rubrics
- Conferencing
- Journaling
- Portfolios
- Mind Maps
- Graphic Organizers
- Peer Review

The purpose of formative assessment is twofold: it gives students a chance to receive continuous feedback and revise their work, and it offers the school librarian and classroom teacher the chance to use a variety of teaching approaches and to differentiate instruction. Working collaboratively with the classroom teacher, the school librarian identifies benchmarks and indicators to be addressed during a unit of study and determines what instruction students need to achieve these goals. Students contribute to the instructional process by identifying their own knowledge gaps and creating strategies for acquiring needed information. Formative assessments are then embedded in learning tasks, giving the classroom teacher and the school librarian feedback that informs their teaching. After every collaborative unit the school librarian and classroom teacher evaluate how the lesson progressed and discuss strategies for improvement.

Summative assessments are conducted at the end of the learning unit to analyze student progress and the success of the unit. They are often in the form of quizzes, tests, products that reflect what the students have learned, and processes that reflect the skills students have acquired. Summative assessments are most often administered by educators, but students can participate in them through self-assessment. In such cases, it is advisable to combine formative assessments. For example, portfolios and conferencing may provide summative data.

The school librarian and classroom teacher engage in reflective practice when they continuously collect evidence of successful teaching and learning. The following contain evidence that indicates strengths and weaknesses of the unit (1) their observations, (2) their notes, logs, or journals, (3) student work as evidenced by formative assessments, and (4) a student survey, written or oral, at the end of the unit. The school librarian and classroom teacher share this evidence at debriefing meetings and record revisions to be made in the unit. The school librarian retains these notes and uses them as part of the planning session the next time he or she collaborates with the teacher.

Student assessments are also used as data or evidence for program planning. The school librarian keeps track of any weaknesses in the instructional design and evaluates how they may be improved through such means as instructional training, collection development, or the purchase of technology tools.

BUILDING THE LEARNING ENVIRONMENT

GUIDELINES

1. The school library program is built on a long-term strategic plan that reflects the mission, goals, and objectives of the school.

2. The school library program has a minimum of one full-time certified/licensed school librarian supported by qualified staff sufficient for the school's instructional programs, services, facilities, size, and number of teachers and students.

3. The school library program includes flexible and equitable access to physical and virtual collections of resources that support the school curriculum and meet the diverse needs of all learners.

4. The school library program has sufficient funding to support priorities and make steady progress to attain the program's mission, goals, and objectives.

5. The school library program includes policies, procedures, and guidelines that support equitable access to ideas and information throughout the school community.

6. The school library program includes a well-developed collection of books, periodicals, and non-print material in a variety of formats that support curricular topics and are suited to inquiry learning and users' needs and interests.

7. The school library program is guided by an advocacy plan that builds support from decision makers who affect the quality of the school library program.

8. The school library program includes support for school librarian and teacher professional development to sustain and increase knowledge and skills.

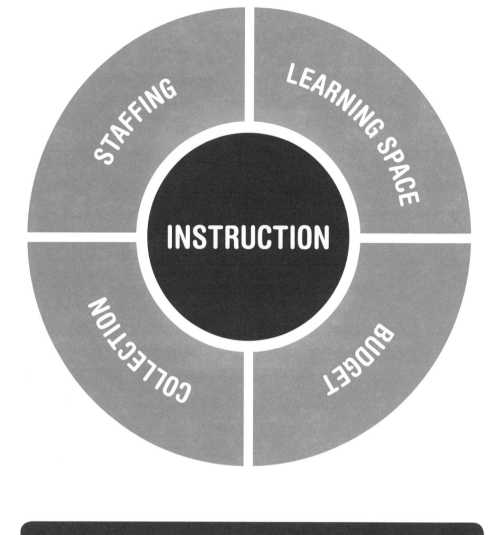

I. PLANNING AND EVALUATING THE SCHOOL LIBRARY PROGRAM

GUIDELINE: The school library program is built on a long-term strategic plan that reflects the mission, goals, and objectives of the school.

ACTIONS: The school librarian:

– uses strategic planning for the continuous improvement of the program

– develops, with input from the school community, mission statements and goals for the school library program that support the mission, goals, and objectives of the school

– conducts ongoing evaluation that creates the data needed for strategically planning comprehensive and collaborative long-range goals for program improvement

– analyzes the data and sets priorities articulated as goals

– writes objectives for each goal that include steps to be taken to attain the goal, a timeline, and a method of determining if the objective was attained

- uses evidence of practice, particularly in terms of learning outcomes, to support program goals and planning

- generates evidence in practice that demonstrates the efficacy and relevance of the school library instructional program

- uses action research, a tool of evidence-based practice, to provide methods for collection of evidence and input from users through interviews, surveys, observations, journaling, focus groups, content analysis, and statistics

- uses research findings to inform decision making and teaching practices

- plans for the future through data collection, program evaluation, and strategic planning

The school librarian uses evidence-based practice to develop a strategic plan that identifies the school library program's goals and objectives, and the steps taken to meet these goals. Prior to creating the strategic plan, the school librarian conducts an environmental scan of the demographics and relevant characteristics of the community in which the school is located. The school's vision and mission statements, academic standing, curricular and extracurricular programs, accreditation reports, and district school development plans should also be reviewed.

After performing an environmental scan, the school librarian conducts a needs assessment by gathering data about the current status of the school library program's components, including the facility, staffing, collection and information access, budgeting, and instruction. Quantitative data include surveys, reports, and statistics. Qualitative data are collected through interviews, observation, and journaling, and are represented by figures, drawings, tables, and descriptive narration.

The school librarian analyzes data from the needs evaluation, identifies strengths and weaknesses of the program, and writes an action plan that includes the long-term goals and short-term (annual) objectives, and the monies needed to finance specific components of the program. The goals and objectives of the action plan comprise the bulk of the budget because they are program priorities. The action plan is then communicated to the principal and staff, and monitored for progress.

The strategic planning process is continuous and centers around the frequent collection of data to monitor the progress of the plan's goals and objectives. An action plan spans a defined period of time, during which it is revised and updated according to the progress made each year. An annual report prepared by the school librarian at the end of each year documents progress toward goals and objectives, and is shared with the principal, library staff, and teachers. The school librarian may also wish to prepare a one-page Executive Summary for distribution to additional stakeholders.

DELVE DEEPER

Estrin, J. 2009. *Closing the Innovation Gap: Reigniting the Spark of Creativity in a Global Economy.* New York: McGraw-Hill.

Geitgey, G. A., and A. E. Tepe. 2007. Can you find the evidence-based practice in your school library? *Library Media Connection* 25, no.6, 10–12.

Langhorne, M. J. 2005. Evidence-based practice: Show me the evidence! Using data in support of library media programs. *Knowledge Quest* 33, no.5, 35–37.

Loertscher, D. V., and R. J. Todd. 2003. *We Boost Achievement! Evidence-Based Practice for school library Media Specialists.* Salt Lake City: Hi Willow Research and Publishing.

McGriff, N., C. A. Harvey, L. B. Preddy. 2004. Collecting the data: Program perception. *school library Media Activities Monthly* 20, no.10, 19–20, 45.

Pappas, M. L. 2008. Designing learning for evidence-based practice. *School Library Media Activities Monthly* 24, no.5 (January), 20–23.

Preddy, L. 2008. Research reflections, journaling, and exit slips. *School Library Media Activities Monthly* 25, no.2, 22–23.

Woodward, J. 2009. *Creating the Customer-Driven Academic Library.* Chicago: ALA.

DELVE DEEPER

Fontichiaro, K. 2008. Staffing has been cut...now what do you do? *School Library Media Activities Monthly* 24, no.8, 28–30.

II. STAFFING

GUIDELINE: The school library program has a minimum of one full-time certified/licensed librarian supported by qualified staff sufficient for the school's instructional programs, services, facilities, size, and number of teachers and students.

ACTIONS: The school librarian:

– analyzes the instructional program to determine appropriate staffing patterns

– works with administrators to ensure that the program is adequately staffed with professional and supporting staff

– creates an environment of mutual respect and collaboration in which all staff members work toward the common goal of student learning

– writes job descriptions that outline the roles, responsibilities, competencies, and qualifications of library staff, including paraprofessionals, student aides, and community volunteers

– works in collaboration with each staff member to evaluate job descriptions on a regular basis

– provides appropriate training and support for student aides and volunteers

Staffing is structured to support teaching and learning throughout the school community. The numbers and skill sets of support staff and volunteers depends on the school's instructional programs, services, facilities, size, and number of students and teachers. However, an school library program includes at least one full-time certified or licensed school librarian to help integrate the program's missions and goals into all aspects of the school curricula. The entire school's students and staff must have the service of a certified school librarian throughout the school day.

The school librarian participates in the careful selection, training, and evaluation of library media support staff in the school. Job descriptions should be written to focus on how each member of the staff supports student learning. The school librarian integrates the program's goals and objectives into staff duties, identifying tasks required for each activity, and assigning them to building-level library staff. Regular staff evaluations and feedback ensure that each member of the team is actively working to support teaching and learning.

III. THE LEARNING SPACE

GUIDELINE: The school library program includes flexible and equitable access to physical and virtual collections of resources that support the school curriculum and meet the diverse needs of all learners.

ACTIONS: The school librarian:

- creates an environment that is conducive to active and participatory learning, resource-based learning, and collaboration with teaching staff

- ensures that library hours provide optimum access for learners and other members of the school community

- promotes flexible scheduling of the school library facility to allow for efficient and timely integration of resources into the curriculum

- creates a friendly, comfortable, well-lit, aesthetically pleasing, and ergonomic space that is centrally located and well integrated with the rest of the school

- designs learning spaces that accommodate a range of teaching methods, learning tasks, and learning outcomes

- provides space and seating that enhances and encourages technology use, leisure reading and browsing, and use of materials in all formats

- provides sufficient and appropriate shelving and storage of resources

- designs and maintains a library website that provides 24–7 access to digital information resources, instructional interventions, reference services, links to other libraries and academic sites, information for parents, and exhibits of exemplary student work

- ensures that technology and telecommunications infrastructure is adequate to support teaching and learning

Open access to the school library's information resources is essential to student learning. Physical access is best achieved through flexible scheduling, in which students and teachers are free to use the library facilities throughout the day. Flexible scheduling allows for collaborative planning and teaching to take place and supports the integration of the school library program into the school, while encouraging student use of the library. Virtual access allows students and teachers to take advantage of the school library's resources after hours and provides continual support for teaching and learning.

DELVE DEEPER

Auld, H. 2002. Combined school-public library facilities: Opinion, case studies, and questions to consider, part 2. *Public Libraries* 41, no.6, 310–16.

Baule, S. M. 2007. *Facility Planning for school library Media and Technology Centers.* Columbus, OH: Linworth Books.

Erikson, R. and C. Markuson. 2007. *Designing a school library Media Center for the Future* (second edition). Chicago: AASL.

Hart, T. L. 2006. *The school library Media Facilities Planner.* New York: Neal-Schuman.

McGregor, J. "Flexible Scheduling: Implementing an Innovation." *School Library Media Research.* <www.ala.org/ala/mgrps/divs/aasl/aaschool library programubsand-journals/slmrb/slmrcon-tents/volume9/flexible.cfm> (accessed February 23, 2009).

Physical Space

The physical space serves as an intellectual gymnasium with multiple, flexible spaces that accommodate a variety of learning tasks. Among such tasks are information seeking, collaborating, and communicating, as well as reading and browsing, and use of multi-media formats. The physical space includes areas for group and independent work, an area for presentations, a multi-media production area, access to an adequate number of workstations, wireless access for students and faculty who bring their own laptops, space for curricular planning and small meetings, ample student research space, and comfortable spaces for reading. Materials are shelved and organized for accessible use by all patrons.

Careful attention is needed when designing or redesigning facilities, including the physical and virtual spaces. Consideration of feedback gathered from students and teachers can help ensure that the physical spaces meet the needs of the school community.

Virtual Space

The Internet has dissolved the physical borders of the library facility. Learners can now access online services, instruction, and references from anywhere and at any time. Thoughtful design of the school library's website can turn this virtual space into a vital instructional tool and resource center, helping the school librarian reach learners who are largely online.

The website connects learners to existing school library services and provides additional services tailored to learners' needs. It should house such materials as scaffolding tools, graphic organizers, downloadable interventions, links to citation sites, reading lists to support projects, and writing guidelines for research papers or reports. By creating pathfinders for specific units of study and posting them on the library website, the school librarian can reach the entire school population. The school librarian may also consider the use of interactive tools, such as wikis and online document-creation sites, which invite collaboration among learners for using resources and production tools.

The flood of online resources can be overwhelming, but they now form a significant part of the collection. Online resources, such as reference materials, media, journals, newspapers, and other information resources, need to be easy for users to find. Whenever possible, federated search tools should be made available and labeled for accessibility, taking into account developmental skills and learning needs. The website should also link to the growing number of live and asynchronous ask-a-librarian services to provide 24–7 help.

IV. THE BUDGET

GUIDELINE: The school library program has sufficient funding to support priorities and make steady progress to attain the program's mission, goals, and objectives.

ACTIONS: The school librarian:

– creates a budget that ensures the library is adequately funded to support the program guidelines

– allocates funding through strategic planning to support priorities and make steady progress to attain outlined goals and objectives

– creates budget rationales and priorities using evidence from strategic planning

– supports the budget with local and nationally published evidence that shows how the school library program impacts learning

– meets regularly with the school principal and/or district chief financial officer to discuss the library budget

– collects current market data about information resource costs and shares the information with decision makers, such as site councils, administrators, and district financial officers

– seeks additional funding through fundraisers, grant writing, and parent donation programs

DELVE DEEPER

Anderson, C. and K. Knop. 2008. Go where the grants are. *Library Media Connection* 27, no.1, 10–14.

Franklin, P., and C. G. Stephens. 2008. Gaining skills to write winning grants. *school library Media Activities Monthly* 25, no.3, 43–44.

Lagesten, C. E. 2007. Students as library leaders: Student team builds leadership skills while helping to battle budget cuts. *Teacher Librarian* 34, no.5, 45–47.

Rosenfeld, E., D. V. Loertscher, eds. 2007. *Toward a 21st Century school library Media Program.* Lanham, MD: Scarecrow.

Tahouri, P. 2005. Winning grants. *Library Media Connection* 24, no.2, 46–47.

Young, R. R. 2008. Eight easy steps to maintain and increase the library media center budget. *Library Media Connection* 26, no.4, 26–27.

The school library program requires solid funding to support teaching and learning throughout the school. Budgets should be outcome-based and present a detailed analysis of how a well-funded program will positively impact students, teachers, and the library program. Improving instruction is the overriding concern when identifying goals and objectives that need funding. Budget goals are also based on the action plan generated through the strategic planning process, and should consider school improvement and development plans, accreditation reports, recommendations from state standards for the school library program, and needs based on implementing the AASL program guidelines. The best way to ensure an optimal school library program budget is to show progress through needs assessment, and goals and objectives in an action plan. These outcomes document the rationale for an increased budget and should be the basis for program evaluation. Addressing such concerns creates support among faculty and generates a better rationale for the budget.

EXAMPLES OF ALTERNATIVE FUNDING SOURCES

- Fundraising events
- Partnerships (with magnet schools and businesses, for example)
- Grants and foundations
- Principal's discretionary budget
- PTA/PTO funds
- Staff development funds
- Local consortia for group discounts and business partnerships
- Department budgets
- Awards from professional organizations

A well-planned budget can help counteract shrinking monies by effectively using available funds and tracking legislative and school district priorities that provide additional revenue resources. Creative planning, such as opting for free web-based applications and open source software over costly traditional software programs, can help keep the school library's resources current even on a tight budget. Alternative funding sources, such as partnerships and grants, can also supplement the school library program's budget.

The continual process of collecting data and making adjustments to teaching and program administration is key to assessing whether the school library program has met the goals detailed in the action plan. Assessment should focus on how the budget has impacted student learning, including how it has helped to integrate 21st-century learning standards within the curriculum, the role of information technology in the school, the quality of facilities and resources, and the quality and relevance of policies and procedures.

V. POLICIES

GUIDELINE: The school library program includes policies, procedures, and guidelines that support equitable access to ideas and information throughout the school community.

ACTIONS: The school librarian:

– seeks input from appropriate members of the school community when developing policies

– develops and implements board-approved collection development policies, including those for selection and purchasing

– works with the technology department and school administrators to develop and implement acceptable-use policies

– works with faculty to develop policies that guide the ethical use of information

– establishes school library program acquisition, processing, and cataloging procedures that conform with district policies

– establishes policies and procedures for the circulation of library materials

– establishes policies for reserving and scheduling use of library spaces and resources

– works in conjunction with other school library professionals in the district to establish a reconsideration policy for challenged materials, which is adopted by the local board of education

DELVE DEEPER

Bishop, K. 2007. *The Collection Program in Schools: Concepts, Practices, and Information Sources*, 4th ed. Westport, CT: Libraries Unlimited.

Dickinson, G., K. Gavigan, and S. Pribesh. 2008. "Open and Accessible: The Relationship between Closures and Circulation in School Library Media Centers." *School Library Media Research*, vol 11. <www.ala.org/ala/mgrps/divs/aasl/ aaschool library programubsand-journals/slmrb/slmrcon-tents/volume11/contents.cfm> (accessed February 23, 2009).

Hoffmann, F. W. and R. J. Wood. 2007. *Library Collection Development Policies: School Libraries and Learning Resource Centers*. New York: Scarecrow.

The establishment of policies and procedures guides the acquisition, use, and review of information resources for the entire school community. To ensure that policies and procedures reflect the current legal and ethical principles underlying information access, intellectual property rights, and the use of information technology, the school librarian must stay abreast of current research and legislation regarding these issues. All policies, such as circulation policies, privacy policies, acceptable-use policies, and rules and guidelines for student behavior, are developed collaboratively with stakeholders.

Intellectual freedom is a core value of the library profession and should be reflected in all school library policies. Learners have the right to a relevant, balanced, and diverse school library collection that represents all points of view. The school librarian assumes a leadership role in protecting minors' First Amendment right to read and to receive information and ideas. The school librarian should base policies on the principles of librarianship expressed in the *Code of Ethics of the American Library Association*, and in the Association's *Library Bill of Rights and Interpretations of the Library Bill of Rights*. These documents, which appear in the appendices of this publication, serve to guide librarians on issues of intellectual freedom that arise over access and use of electronic information, services, and networks.

The multitude of online resources has made it easy for anyone to copy information with a simple click of the mouse. In addition, the culture of sharing content and building on others' work, while often beneficial to creative and collaborative work, has made copyright issues more complicated. A number of learners are now content creators, as well as consumers, and they must be informed of their intellectual property rights and knowledgeable about acceptable-use guidelines. As an information specialist, the school librarian must lead the way in promoting academic honesty by working with the principal, faculty members, and the district administration to create a school integrity policy that includes guidelines for proper use of information and a clear definition of plagiarism.

VI. COLLECTION AND INFORMATION ACCESS

GUIDELINE: The school library program includes a well-developed collection of books, periodicals, and non-print material in a variety of formats that support curricular topics and are suited to inquiry learning and users' needs and interests.

ACTIONS: The school librarian:

– collaborates with the teaching staff to develop an up-to-date collection of print and digital resources in multiple genres that appeals to differences in age, gender, ethnicity, reading abilities, and information needs

– advocates for and protects intellectual access to information and ideas

– maps the collection to ensure that it meets the needs of the school curriculum

– regularly seeks input from students through such tools as surveys and suggestion boxes to determine students' reading interests and motivations

– ensures the collection is centralized and decentralized as needed to support classroom activities and other learning initiatives in the school

– promotes alternative reading options through reading lists, bibliographies, and webliographies that include periodicals, bestseller lists, graphic novels, books, and websites in multiple languages

- links the digital library to local, regional, or state online networks, connecting with other public or academic libraries to take advantage of available virtual resources to support the school curriculum

- tracks inventory in the school library, taking advantage of up-to-date automation systems and keeping current with software releases and training

- conducts regular weeding to ensure that the library collection is up to date

- reviews challenged materials using the reconsideration policy

Collection and information access in the school library support teaching and learning by providing diverse sources of information that match curricular needs, lend themselves to units of inquiry, and are of high interest to students. The school librarian works collaboratively with classroom teachers in selecting materials. Professional reviews aid the school librarian and classroom teachers in making appropriate purchasing decisions.

One of the challenges faced by the school librarian in developing the collection is selecting the appropriate format for resources. When making choices between print and digital resources, the school librarian must decide which format best suits curricular purposes, student needs, the budget, and the particular circumstances of the school library. For example, with an adequate number of workstations, electronic materials are more scalable than print resources, providing continuous remote access. The creation of a collection development action plan that uses virtual and physical resources wisely can help guide the acquisition of resources.

The school librarian subscribes to local, state, or regional online networks to take advantage of available virtual resources that provide educators with fast and easy access to age-appropriate materials aligned to the state's education curriculum. These information networks support teaching and learning by providing equitable access to quality resources for promoting information literacy and media literacy through the use of technology. Cooperative purchasing or resource-sharing arrangements are available in many states. In addition to providing access to curriculum-related materials, statewide online databases may support library automation for school libraries with individual school Web catalogs, and include materials that support

DELVE DEEPER

Adams, H. R. 2008. *Ensuring Intellectual Freedom and Access to Information in the school library Media Program.* Westport, CT: Libraries Unlimited.

American Library Association. 2006. *Intellectual Freedom Manual.* 7th ed. Chicago: ALA.

Barr, C. 2008. *Best New Media, K–12: A guide to movies, subscription web sites, and educational software and games.* Westport, CT: Libraries Unlimited.

Barstow, B., J. Riggle, and L. Molnar. 2008. *Beyond Picture Books: Subject Access to Best Books for Beginning Readers.* Westport, CT: Libraries Unlimited.

Kerby, R. N. 2006. *Collection Development for the school library Media Program: A Beginner's Guide.* Chicago: ALA.

Kern, K. 2009. *Virtual Reference Best Practices: Tailoring Services to Your Library.* Chicago: ALA.

Scales, P. R. for OIF. 2009. *Protecting Intellectual Freedom in Your School Library.* Chicago: ALA.

FACTORS TO CONSIDER WHEN BUILDING THE VIRTUAL COLLECTION

- **How much access to computers do learners have in the school library, in the rest of the school, at home, and in the community?**

- **When asked, which resources do users request?**

- **How important is providing access to the information from outside the school or by multiple simultaneous users?**

professional development for educators, digital video collections, instructions on site navigation, as well as materials for parents to support learning at home. Through marketing and public relations efforts, school library programs at centers participating in statewide networks must ensure that students, teachers, administrators, and parents are aware of these resources and know how to use them.

As the scope and size of the collection depends on each individual library's patrons and their needs, no quantitative measures can apply to all school librarys. However, many tools, such as state and national program surveys and reports, enable the school librarian to benchmark the collection and other aspects of the program. AASL's *School Libraries Count!*, a national survey of school library programs, includes statistics on library collections and total expenditures per student, among other topics <www.ala.org/aasl/slcsurvey>.

The school librarian advocates for access to a broad range of ideas and information for all members of the learning community. This includes students who do not have computer access at home. Even in a school or other public setting, learners may not have access to propriety software or equivalent open source alternatives, or access to filtered Web resources. The school librarian ensures that students with special needs have access to adaptive technology, as well as to mainstream resources, so they can enjoy equivalent learning experiences.

Student access to information and new tools for accessing and communicating information is more necessary and more complicated in a political environment motivated by fear and concern for online safety. In such an environment, the school librarian defends students' freedom to read and their freedom to make informed decisions. To do so, the school librarian must be informed about legislation that may restrict information access in schools. The school librarian is a team member who evaluates the acceptable-use policy of the school and/or district to ensure that it recognizes new and emerging technologies, and considers differentiated strategies for elementary, middle, and high school students.

The selection policy and collection development plans are used to regularly evaluate the collection. The school librarian uses data to build a rationale for funding and to evaluate the usefulness of the collection for promoting reading. Electronic tools can help in the assessment and development of the collection, and automated library management programs can provide statistics on use.

VII. OUTREACH

GUIDELINE: The school library program is guided by an advocacy plan that builds support from decision makers who affect the quality of the school library program.

ACTIONS: The school librarian:

– analyzes stakeholder goals and issues for potential alignment with library activities and resources, and builds promotional efforts around them

– builds relationships with local, state, and national decision makers

– forms partnerships with the local and global community to promote student learning

– uses local, state, national, and international school library data to engage support

– forms a "Friends of the school library" program

– encourages parents and community members to support learners by volunteering in the library

– participates in PTA/PTO or other school-based parent groups

– offers to provide informational programs for community special-interest and service groups

– encourages visits to and use of the library by parents, administrators, elected officials, and other stakeholders

– attends department, curriculum, faculty, and other school- and district-based meetings

– communicates to stakeholders through the library website, parent newsletters, e-mail, and other formats

– writes articles and regular reports giving concrete evidence of what the library does to prepare learners to be successful in the twenty-first century

DELVE DEEPER

Church, A. "The Instructional Role of the Library Media Specialist as Perceived by Elementary School Principals."<www.ala.org/ala/mgrps/divs/aasl/aaschool library programub-sandjournals/slmrb/slmrcontents/volume11/church.cfm?> (accessed February 23, 2009).

Fichtman, N. D. and D. Yendol-Hoppey. 2008. *The Reflective Educator's Guide to Professional Development: Coaching Inquiry-Oriented Learning Communities.* Thousand Oaks, CA: Corwin.

Spector, J. 2008. *We Are Smarter Than Me: How to Unleash the Power of Crowds in Your Business.* Philadelphia: Wharton School Publishing.

Williams, B. R. 2008. *Twelve Roles of Facilitators for School Change,* 2nd ed. Thousand Oaks, CA: Corwin.

Woolls, B. 2008. *The school library Media Manager,* 4th ed. Westport, CT: Libraries Unlimited.

School library services are sometimes undervalued when in fact they are needed more than ever. Though the Web has increased the importance of information-seeking and evaluation skills, many members of the school community have misconceptions about the Web and the information it offers. The school librarian must advocate for the vital role that school library programs play in teaching and learning. To do so, he or she must create a common agenda with school and education decision makers, and develop community partnerships and collaborations.

Advocacy is an ongoing process of building partnerships, and begins with a vision and a plan for the school library program that is then matched to the agenda and priorities of stakeholders. Advocacy involves a combination of public relations efforts—one-way communication to promote who we are, what we do, when and where we do it, and for whom—and marketing, a planned and sustained process to assess the customer's needs, and then to select materials and services to meet those needs.

Advocacy initiatives are rooted in the evidence generated by needs assessments and action plans. Instead of focusing on what the school library program does, evidence-based advocacy focuses on what students learn. Ongoing data collection informs the program and helps the school librarian identify best practices. Formative assessment tools, such as journaling, portfolios, standards-based scoring guides and rubrics, recorded observations, student interviews, surveys, and focus groups, can be used. Summative assessments, including statewide test results, are also valuable. After reviewing data, the school librarian reflects on how the program can improve and evaluates how the program impacts student achievement.

The modes of advocacy should address issues that emerge from needs assessments, which are used to establish program goals and objectives. The goals and objectives are articulated in an action plan that is, in effect, an instrument of evidence-based advocacy. Support for the programming plan is developed with students, staff, administrators, and parents as members of the school community. The school librarian then develops strategies, identifying potential obstacles, a timetable, the parties involved, and the steps to be taken to achieve the goals. When advocacy is focused on particular needs of the school library program, evidence of those needs provide strong rationales for increased resources.

VIII. PROFESSIONAL DEVELOPMENT

GUIDELINE: The school library program includes support for school librarian and teacher professional development to sustain and increase knowledge and skills.

ACTIONS: The school librarian:

– ensures access to professional development opportunities for professional and paraprofessional staff

– participates in and provides professional development to sustain and to develop knowledge and skills

– seeks opportunities to teach new skills to the faculty and staff, whether in a classroom setting or one-on-one instruction

– takes advantage of professional development opportunities and shares new learning with the school administration and faculty

– participates in local, regional, state, and national educational conferences as a learner and as a teacher

– reads research relevant to school libraries, student learning, and new developments in the educational field

Working collaboratively with classroom teachers, the school librarian develops a long-term plan for professional development that links to improving student achievement. This professional development involves setting personal learning goals, connecting research and practice, and modeling good teaching strategies. Through regular assessment of the school library program, the school librarian can determine aspects of the program that may be strengthened through training or other support. The school librarian should provide resources, activities, and other learning opportunities to staff. Professional development also takes place informally through ongoing sharing of ideas between the school librarian, teachers, and students.

Though professional conferences and workshops still have their place in professional development, the school librarian must also provide staff with opportunities for participatory, hands-on learning. For example, learning how to use a new technology tool becomes much more meaningful when participants are able to hold the gadget in their hands and try it out for themselves. Participating in virtual discussion groups can help make professional growth a continual process and offer time for reflection on ways to aid student learning.

DELVE DEEPER

Bush, G. Inquiry groups for professional development and information literacy instruction. *school library Media Activities Monthly* 24, no.10, 39–43.

Cameron, G., M. McIver, and R. Goddard. 2008. A different kind of community. *Changing Schools* 57 (Winter), 6–7. <www.mcrel.org/pdf/changing schools/0125NL_08_Changing Schools_Winter.pdf> (accessed January 14, 2009).

DuFour, R., R. Dufour, and R. Eaker. 2006. *Learning by Doing: A Handbook for Professional Learning Communities at Work.* Bloomington, IN: Solution Tree.

Fontichiaro, K. 2008. Planning an online professional development module. *school library Media Activities Monthly* 25, no.2, 30–31.

Franklin, P., and C. G. Stephens. Professionally speaking: You need a professional collection. *School Library Media Activities Monthly* 24, no.1, 43–44.

Professional training on emerging technologies is now a substantive part of professional development. As information specialists, school librarians must keep abreast of applications for emerging technologies used to find, use, and share information. Technology is now inextricably linked with multiple literacies and with other 21st-century skills needed to succeed in work and in life. Thus, the school librarian must model the use of technology for staff, teachers and other educators, and students, as well as provide professional development to build 21st-century skills throughout the school community.

The visionary school librarian works year-round to stay immersed in the current research and best practices in the field. In addition to attending face-to-face conferences, a school librarian can gain knowledge from conferences by accessing keynotes, PowerPoint presentations, and podcasts online, or by attending virtual conferences. Active membership in professional organizations, regular reading of professional and technology journals, and participation in online learning communities are just a few examples of how the school librarian can stay current on the latest issues and ideas surrounding effective planning and teaching strategies.

 **EMPOWERING LEARNING THROUGH LEADERSHIP**

"If we are to retain our school library programs and expand them across the country, it will be critical that more people in the profession take up that leadership charge in their buildings! Our roles may continue to change and alter as more technology and information tools become available. Flexibility will be important as we continue to move beyond the keeper of the books to the facilitator that helps guide our students through the jungle of information."

— AASL survey participant

GUIDELINE: The school library program is built by professionals who model leadership and best practice for the school community.

ACTIONS: The school librarian:

– is a visible and active leader within the school community

– is an early adopter of changes in current educational and technology trends

– serves on the decision-making team of the school

– benchmarks program to school, state, and national educational program standards

– participates in local, regional, state, and national professional associations for education and librarianship

– shares knowledge about libraries and learning by publishing articles in the school newsletter or other community news sources

– shares expertise by presenting information at faculty meetings, parent meetings, and school board meetings

– shares best practices and research by publishing articles in state and national professional journals

– uses research to inform practice and makes evidence-based decisions

– takes responsibility for professional growth through continuous program improvement

– fosters an atmosphere of respect and rapport between the school librarian and all members of the learning community to encourage student learning and to promote teacher enthusiasm and participation

– creates an environment that is conducive to active and participatory learning, resource-based learning, and collaboration with teaching staff

45

DELVE DEEPER

Carr, J., ed. (for AASL). 2008. *Leadership for Excellence: Insights of the National school library Media Program of the Year Award Winners.* Chicago: ALA Editions.

Donham, J. 2008. *Enhancing Teaching and Learning: A Leadership Guide for school librarians*, 2nd ed. New York: Neal-Schuman.

Fullan, M. 2008. *The Six Secrets of Change: What the Best Leaders Do to Help Their Organizations Survive and Thrive.* Hoboken, NJ: Jossey Bass.

Hord, S. M. and W. A. Sommers. 2008. *Leading Professional Learning Communities: Voices From Research and Practice.* Thousand Oaks, CA: Corwin.

Lance, K. and D. V. Loertscher. 2005. *Powering Achievement*, 3rd ed. Salt Lake City: Hi Willow Research and Publishing.

Perrault, A. M. 2007. Schools as information ecologies: A proposed framework of study. *School Libraries Worldwide* 13, no.2, 49–62.

It is both a challenging and an exciting time to be a member of the school library profession. The tools we can use to connect users to information are continually multiplying. The skills we teach students are vital to their success as learners and users of information. However, the profession remains challenged by misconceptions about the school librarian's role in teaching and learning. Leading librarians embrace these challenges and opportunities to empower learning through their roles as instructional partners, information specialists, teachers, and program administrators.

Educators are at a crossroads in determining how to bring schools into the twenty-first century and ensure that learners develop the skills necessary to succeed in work and in life. Many agree that multiple literacies, including information, media, and technology literacies, are the foundation on which high-level thinking skills are built. School librarians must play a leading role in weaving such skills throughout the curriculum so that all members of the school community are effective users of ideas and information (Carr 2008).

I. Leadership in a Global Society

Many schools in the United States still embody a 20th-century industrial model that focuses on individual learning and the memorization of facts rather than on the development of high-level thinking, problem-solving skills, and collaborative work. Outside school walls, the new environment represented by peer-to-peer sharing, globalization, and easy access to information and resources has sparked a revolution in the way we live. In *Wikinomics: How Mass Collaboration Changes Everything*, Don Tapscott and Anthony D. Williams describe how the new technology landscape has transformed business and social models.

"These changes, among others, are ushering us toward a world where knowledge, power, and productive capability will be more dispersed than at any time in our history—a world where value creation will be fast, fluid, and persistently disruptive. A world where only the connected will survive. A power shift is underway, and a tough new business rule is emerging: Harness the new collaboration or perish. Those who fail to grasp this will find themselves ever more isolated—cut off from the networks that are sharing, adapting, and updating knowledge to create value" (Tapscott and Willliams 2008, 12).

As interactive technology has come to permeate every aspect of daily life, leading businesses and organizations have changed the way they work in order to thrive in this new global economy. Likewise, schools must move toward a more connected, collaborative form of leadership. School librarians must lead this revolution to make room for new models of teaching, learning, and organization to prepare learners for this collaborative environment and address the needs of a generation that has grown up participating, not just being broadcast to.

II. Building Relationships

The school library program must offer leadership from a peer level—leadership for both faculty and administrators. This type of leadership is possible when the school librarian develops influence and expertise, and helps the organization develop vision and build capacity. In an organization with many specialties, schools need a leader who has a deep understanding of the roles and needs of others. If the school librarian is to lead, he or she must understand content-area teaching and learning, new pedagogical strategies, trends in the education and technology landscapes, and the skills related to information, media, and technology fluency.

The school librarian's ability to build strong relationships with teachers, school administrators, and the community is key to implementing change. To build such relationships, the school librarian must become a highly visible member of the school community. Active participation in faculty councils, grade level and department meetings, and decisions that affect student learning are just a few ways the school librarian can ensure that the school reflects learning practices that build 21st-century skills. The school librarian should be a leading member of school-wide committees to contribute expertise on such issues as curriculum development, use of technology, equity of information access, intellectual freedom, and intellectual property rights, among others.

CURRICULUM COMMITTEE: The school librarian joins committees that make curriculum decisions on district, school, or department levels to participate in decision making and to work with colleagues to improve the quality of instruction. Knowledge of school-wide policies and decisions informs the school librarian's design, delivery, and assessment of instructional practices in collaboration with colleagues.

TECHNOLOGY COMMITTEE: The school librarian serves on the building and district level committee, offering research services to support the work of the committee as well as information about students' technology use and needs.

POLICY COMMITTEE: The school librarian serves on committees to offer expertise on academic integrity, documentation, and information and technology use policies.

STAFF DEVELOPMENT COMMITTEE: The school librarian helps plan whole-school professional development efforts, especially those involved with improving reading, writing, research, and the integration of technology.

Classroom teachers and administrators are often unaware of the role the school library program plays in advancing student achievement. Thus, the school librarian must use a variety of communication tools to make library services visible to administrators, teachers, students, and parents. Writing articles for the school newspaper and the parent/PTA newsletter, posting library news on the library website, sending out e-mails to the school staff about library activities or topics that concern the faculty, and alerting administration to noteworthy events in the school library are examples of how the school librarian can increase awareness of the school library's role in student learning.

Developing connections with families and community stakeholders is vital to integrating the school library program into the school curriculum. The school librarian meets with teachers and parents to encourage their involvement in the program and to ensure that their needs are being addressed. Through networking opportunities at conferences, social networking websites, and other virtual spaces, the school librarian also communicates with leaders beyond the building level who share interests in learning and technologies.

III. Characteristics of Good Leadership

In all professions, strong leaders embody certain qualities that draw people to them and make them work toward achieving a common goal. Leaders are passionate about their work and look for new ideas in all their experiences, both personal and professional. They are excellent communicators who instill enthusiasm in others by making them feel that they are important members of a team. Strong leaders foster an environment of creativity, innovation, and openness to new ideas. They welcome and encourage input from others to create a consensus about the best way forward. They look ahead to future obstacles and continually retool to meet challenges.

Leading school librarians create an environment where collaboration and creative problem solving thrive. They continuously strive to advance their skills by reading professional journals and books, attending conferences, and networking with other librarians. District school librarians should meet regularly to share ideas, issues, and new strategies and tools, and to plan future services. Such meetings are critical to ensure the entire department has an opportunity to grow and retool. School librarians who are not part of a school district can find (or start) a local school library consortium.

IV. Planning Our Future

The shifting, interactive information landscape is riper than ever for assumption of leadership strategies by information professionals. School librarians must expand their leadership capacity and position themselves to meet emerging challenges. To do so, they must have a long-term vision of what they wish to accomplish with their programs. Only through the development of an articulated mission and long-range plan will school librarians be able to implement an effective school library program that positively impacts student achievement. By continuously reflecting on our progress and retooling as necessary, school librarians can lead the way in building a learning environment that supports development of the skills learners need to be active members of our global society.

CHARACTERISTICS OF GOOD LEADERSHIP

- Being creative

- Being interactive

- Being vision-headed

- Empowering others (by encouraging participation and involvement)

- Being passionate about your work

Source: Hackman and Johnson 2003

APPENDICES

APPENDIX A:
The American Library Association's (ALA) Core Competencies of Librarianship

This document defines the basic knowledge to be possessed by all persons graduating from an ALA-accredited master's program in library and information studies. Librarians working in school, academic, public, special, and governmental libraries, and in other contexts will need to possess specialized knowledge beyond that specified here.

CONTENTS

1. Foundations of the Profession
2. Information Resources
3. Organization of Recorded Knowledge and Information
4. Technological Knowledge and Skills
5. Reference and User Services
6. Research
7. Continuing Education and Lifelong Learning
8. Administration and Management

A person graduating from an ALA-accredited master's program in library and information studies should know and, where appropriate, be able to employ:

1. Foundations of the Profession

1A. The ethics, values, and foundational principles of the library and information profession.

1B. The role of library and information professionals in the promotion of democratic principles and intellectual freedom (including freedom of expression, thought, and conscience).

1C. The history of libraries and librarianship.

1D. The history of human communication and its impact on libraries.

1E. Current types of library (school, public, academic, special, etc.) and closely related information agencies.

1F. National and international social, public, information, economic, and cultural policies and trends of significance to the library and information profession.

1G. The legal framework within which libraries and information agencies operate. That framework includes laws relating to copyright, privacy, freedom of expression, equal rights (e.g., the Americans with Disabilities Act), and intellectual property.

1H. The importance of effective advocacy for libraries, librarians, other library workers, and library services.

1I. The techniques used to analyze complex problems and create appropriate solutions.

1J. Effective communication techniques (verbal and written).

1K. Certification and/or licensure requirements of specialized areas of the profession.

2. Information Resources

2A. Concepts and issues related to the lifecycle of recorded knowledge and information, from creation through various stages of use to disposition.

2B. Concepts, issues, and methods related to the acquisition and disposition of resources, including evaluation, selection, purchasing, processing, storing, and de-selection.

2C. Concepts, issues, and methods related to the management of various collections.

2C. Concepts, issues, and methods related to the maintenance of collections, including preservation and conservation.

3. Organization of Recorded Knowledge and Information

3A. The principles involved in the organization and representation of recorded knowledge and information.

3B. The developmental, descriptive, and evaluative skills needed to organize recorded knowledge and information resources.

3C. The systems of cataloging, metadata, indexing, and classification standards and methods used to organize recorded knowledge and information.

4. Technological Knowledge and Skills

4A. Information, communication, assistive, and related technologies as they affect the resources, service delivery, and uses of libraries and other information agencies.

4B. The application of information, communication, assistive, and related technology and tools consistent with professional ethics and prevailing service norms and applications.

4C. The methods of assessing and evaluating the specifications, efficacy, and cost efficiency of technology-based products and services.

4C. The principles and techniques necessary to identify and analyze emerging technologies and innovations in order to recognize and implement relevant technological improvements.

5. Reference and User Services

5A. The concepts, principles, and techniques of reference and user services that provide access to relevant and accurate recorded knowledge and information to individuals of all ages and groups.

5B. Techniques used to retrieve, evaluate, and synthesize information from diverse sources for use by individuals of all ages and groups.

5C. The methods used to interact successfully with individuals of all ages and groups to provide consultation, mediation, and guidance in their use of recorded knowledge and information.

5D. Information literacy/information competence techniques and methods, numerical literacy, and statistical literacy.

5E. The principles and methods of advocacy used to reach specific audiences to promote and explain concepts and services.

5F. The principles of assessment and response to diversity in user needs, user communities, and user preferences.

5G. The principles and methods used to assess the impact of current and emerging situations or circumstances on the design and implementation of appropriate services or resource development.

6. Research

6A. The fundamentals of quantitative and qualitative research methods.

6B. The central research findings and research literature of the field.

6C. The principles and methods used to assess the actual and potential value of new research.

7. Continuing Education and Lifelong Learning

7A. The necessity of continuing professional development of practitioners in libraries and other information agencies.

7B. The role of the library in the lifelong learning of patrons, including an understanding of lifelong learning in the provision of quality service and the use of lifelong learning in the promotion of library services.

7C. Learning theories, instructional methods, and achievement measures; and their application in libraries and other information agencies.

7D. The principles related to the teaching and learning of concepts, processes and skills used in seeking, evaluating, and using recorded knowledge and information.

8. Administration and Management

8A. The principles of planning and budgeting in libraries and other information agencies.

8B. The principles of effective personnel practices and human resource development.

8C. The concepts behind, and methods for, assessment and evaluation of library services and their outcomes.

8D. The concepts behind, and methods for, developing partnerships, collaborations, networks, and other structures with all stakeholders and within communities served.

8E. The concepts behind, issues relating to, and methods for, principled, transformational leadership.

Approved and adopted as policy by the ALA Council, January 27, 2009.

APPENDIX B: Library Bill of Rights

The American Library Association affirms that all libraries are forums for information and ideas, and that the following basic policies should guide their services.

I. Books and other library resources should be provided for the interest, information, and enlightenment of all people of the community the library serves. Materials should not be excluded because of the origin, background, or views of those contributing to their creation.

II. Libraries should provide materials and information presenting all points of view on current and historical issues. Materials should not be proscribed or removed because of partisan or doctrinal disapproval.

III. Libraries should challenge censorship in the fulfillment of their responsibility to provide information and enlightenment.

IV. Libraries should cooperate with all persons and groups concerned with resisting abridgment of free expression and free access to ideas.

V. A person's right to use a library should not be denied or abridged because of origin, age, background, or views.

VI. Libraries which make exhibit spaces and meeting rooms available to the public they serve should make such facilities available on an equitable basis, regardless of the beliefs or affiliations of individuals or groups requesting their use.

Adopted June 18, 1948, by the ALA Council; amended February 2, 1961; amended June 28, 1967; amended January 23, 1980; inclusion of "age" reaffirmed January 24, 1996. A full history of this statement is included in American Library Association, *Intellectual Freedom Manual*, 7th ed. (Chicago: ALA, 2006). For more documents, visit http://www.ala.org/oif and look at the documents related to the Library Bill of Rights.

APPENDIX C:
Access to Resources and Services in the School Library Media Program: An Interpretation of the Library Bill of Rights

The school library media program plays a unique role in promoting intellectual freedom. It serves as a point of voluntary access to information and ideas and as a learning laboratory for students as they acquire critical thinking and problem-solving skills needed in a pluralistic society. Although the educational level and program of the school necessarily shape the resources and services of a school library media program, the principles of the Library Bill of Rights apply equally to all libraries, including school library media programs. Under these principles, all students have equitable access to library facilities, resources, and instructional programs.

School library media specialists assume a leadership role in promoting the principles of intellectual freedom within the school by providing resources and services that create and sustain an atmosphere of free inquiry. School library media specialists work closely with teachers to integrate instructional activities in classroom units designed to equip students to locate, evaluate, and use a broad range of ideas effectively. Intellectual freedom is fostered by educating students in the use of critical thinking skills to empower them to pursue free inquiry responsibly and independently. Through resources, programming, and educational processes, students and teachers experience the free and robust debate characteristic of a democratic society.

School library media specialists cooperate with other individuals in building collections of resources that meet the needs as well as the developmental and maturity levels of students. These collections provide resources that support the mission of the school district and are consistent with its philosophy, goals, and objectives. Resources in school library media collections are an integral component of the curriculum and represent diverse points of view on both current and historical issues. These resources include materials that support the intellectual growth, personal development, individual interests, and recreational needs of students.

While English is, by history and tradition, the customary language of the United States, the languages in use in any given community may vary. Schools serving communities in which other languages are used make efforts to accommodate the needs of students for whom English is a second language. To support these efforts, and to ensure equitable access to resources and services, the school library media program provides resources that reflect the linguistic pluralism of the community.

Members of the school community involved in the collection development process employ educational criteria to select resources unfettered by their personal, political, social, or religious views. Students and educators served by the school library media program have access to resources and services free of constraints resulting from personal, partisan, or doctrinal disapproval. School library media specialists resist efforts by individuals or groups to define what is appropriate for all students or teachers to read, view, hear, or access via electronic means.

Major barriers between students and resources include but are not limited to imposing age, grade-level, or reading-level restrictions on the use of resources; limiting the use of interlibrary loan and access to electronic information; charging fees for information in specific formats; requiring permission from parents or teachers; establishing restricted shelves or closed collections; and labeling. Policies, procedures, and rules related to the use of resources and services support free and open access to information.

It is the responsibility of the governing board to adopt policies that guarantee students access to a broad range of ideas. These include policies on collection development and procedures for the review of resources about which concerns have been raised. Such policies, developed by persons in the school community, provide for a timely and fair hearing and assure that procedures are applied equitably to all expressions of concern. It is the responsibility of school library media specialists to implement district policies and procedures in the school to ensure equitable access to resources and services for all students.

Adopted July 2, 1986, by the ALA Council; amended January 10, 1990; July 12, 2000; January 19, 2005; July 2, 2008. A full history of this statement is included in American Library Association, *Intellectual Freedom Manual*, 7th ed. (Chicago: ALA, 2006). For more documents, visit http://www.ala.org/oif and look at the documents related to the Library Bill of Rights.

APPENDIX D:
Code of Ethics of the American Library Association

As members of the American Library Association, we recognize the importance of codifying and making known to the profession and to the general public the ethical principles that guide the work of librarians, other professionals providing information services, library trustees and library staffs.

Ethical dilemmas occur when values are in conflict. The American Library Association Code of Ethics states the values to which we are committed, and embodies the ethical responsibilities of the profession in this changing information environment.

We significantly influence or control the selection, organization, preservation, and dissemination of information. In a political system grounded in an informed citizenry, we are members of a profession explicitly committed to intellectual freedom and the freedom of access to information. We have a special obligation to ensure the free flow of information and ideas to present and future generations.

The principles of this Code are expressed in broad statements to guide ethical decision making. These statements provide a framework; they cannot and do not dictate conduct to cover particular situations.

I. We provide the highest level of service to all library users through appropriate and usefully organized resources; equitable service policies; equitable access; and accurate, unbiased, and courteous responses to all requests.

II. We uphold the principles of intellectual freedom and resist all efforts to censor library resources.

III. We protect each library user's right to privacy and confidentiality with respect to information sought or received and resources consulted, borrowed, acquired, or transmitted.

IV. We respect intellectual property rights and advocate balance between the interests of information users and rights holders.

V. We treat co-workers and other colleagues with respect, fairness, and good faith, and advocate conditions of employment that safeguard the rights and welfare of all employees of our institutions.

VI. We do not advance private interests at the expense of library users, colleagues, or our employing institutions.

VII. We distinguish between our personal convictions and professional duties and do not allow our personal beliefs to interfere with fair representation of the aims of our institutions or the provision of access to their information resources.

VIII. We strive for excellence in the profession by maintaining and enhancing our own knowledge and skills, by encouraging the professional development of co-workers, and by fostering the aspirations of potential members of the profession.

Adopted June 28, 1997, by the ALA Council; amended January 22, 2008. A full history of this statement is included in American Library Association, *Intellectual Freedom Manual*, 7th ed. (Chicago: ALA, 2006). For more documents, visit http://www.ala.org/oif and look at the documents related to the Library Bill of Rights.

APPENDIX E:
A History of School Library Program Standards and Guidelines*

1917 Standard High School Library Organization for Accredited Secondary Schools of Different Sizes, Symposium on a Standard Library Equipment for High Schools Contributed by Leaders in the Movement for Better High School Libraries, presented at a meeting of the North Central Association of Colleges and Secondary Schools March 21–24, 1917. C.C. Certain, chairman [a draft document which later became the 1918 Standards]

1918 Standard Library Organization and Equipment for Secondary Schools of Different Sizes Report of the Committee on Library Organization and Equipment, National Education Association, Proceedings of the National Educational Association, 1918 p.691–719. C.C. Certain, chairman

1918 Standard Library Organization and Equipment for Secondary Schools of Different Sizes National Education Association, Department of Secondary Education, 1918. C.C. Certain, chairman. [Comment: these are the same as the 1918 proceedings, but published separately and later endorsed by ALA in 1920.]

1920 Standard Library Organization and Equipment for Secondary Schools Published by the New York State Library, Library School Bulletin 45, University of the State of New York, 1920. [A reprint of the 1918 Standards with notes particular to NYS certification and Regents policy]

*Adapted from Frances Roscello's *President's Column* in *Knowledge Quest*, vol. 32, no. 4 (March/April 2004).

1925 Elementary School Library Standards

Report of the Joint Committee on Elementary School Library Standards, 1925. C.C. Certain, chairman [Joint Committee of the NEA Department of Elementary School Principals and ALA School Librarians' Section]

1939 Evaluation Criteria

Cooperative Study of Secondary School Standards, The Middle States Association of Colleges and Secondary Schools, 1939 & 1950.

1945 School Libraries for Today and Tomorrow: Functions and Standards

American Library Association, Committees on Post-War Planning, Divisions of Libraries for Children and Young People and American Association of School Librarians, 1945. Mary Peacock Douglas, chairman.

1954 School Library Standards

U.S. Department of Health, Education, and Welfare, Office of Education, 1954. Nora E. Beust, editor [A review and history of standards and regulations, including a survey of the states, not a new set of standards]

1960 Standards for School Library Programs

American Association of School Librarians, a Division of the American Library Association, in cooperation with [nineteen educational organizations], 1960

1969 Standards for School Media Programs

American Association of School Librarians, a Division of the American Library Association, and the Department of Audiovisual Instruction, a Department of the National Education Association, in cooperation with representatives from [27 educational organizations], 1969.

1975 Media Programs: District and School

American Association of School Librarians, a Division of the American Library Association, and Association for Educational Communications and Technology, 1975

Guidelines for School Library Programs

1988 Information Power: Guidelines for School Library Media Programs

American Association of School Librarians, a Division of the American Library Association, and Association for Educational Communications and Technology, 1988

1998 Information Power: Building Partnerships for Learning

American Association of School Librarians, a Division of the American Library Association, and Association for Educational Communications and Technology, 1998 [includes Information Literacy Standards for Student Learning]

APPENDIX F:
Learning4Life (L4L): A National Plan for Implementation of *Standards for the 21st-Century Learner* and *Empowering Learners: Guidelines for School Library Programs*

This implementation plan was created to support states, school systems, and individual schools preparing to implement the *Standards for the 21st-Century Learner* and *Empowering Learners: Guidelines for School Library Programs.* The plan will also increase awareness and understanding of the learning standards and guidelines and create a committed group of stakeholders with a shared voice.

While the learning standards and guidelines define what "should be" in terms of information literacy, research through guided inquiry, and the integration of technology in the traditional school context, they also acknowledge varied and new forms of teaching and learning in a social and global context. Foundational to this plan is the fundamental value of reading, core content, and mastery of skills that produce deep knowledge and understanding, as well as the portable skills that serve individuals for a lifetime, making them critical thinkers, problem solvers, and continually evolving learners.

To this end, the implementation plan addresses the practical realization of these important skills and values as it:

– identifies guiding principles and an overarching position and branding statement;
– identifies target audiences (internal and external);
– identifies training opportunities and resources;
– provides a communication plan;
– provides a plan for continuous feedback, evaluation, and sustainability;
– provides a plan for endorsements and support;
– provides supporting documents.

The plan is available online at
www.ala.org/aasl/learning4life

APPENDIX G :
Resources for Staying Current in the School Library Field

Data from *School Libraries Count!*, the American Association of School Librarians' Longitudinal Study

The American Association of School Librarians (AASL) launched *School Libraries Count!* in 2007. *School Libraries Count!* is a longitudinal study being used to track changes in the school library field so that the association can understand the state of school library programs nationally. National estimates are being developed on the basis of survey responses from a stratified random sample of public schools. All K-12 schools, public and private, are invited to participate each year on a voluntary basis.

The annual survey will result in a longitudinal series that will provide data on the health of the nation's school library programs. The survey is gathering information in such areas as school library program staff, activities, scheduling, collections, technology, and expenditures. Each survey also includes a question on a unique topic for just that year. This data will help provide benchmarking data for school library programs.

Survey participants can also access personalized reports comparing their data to other school libraries with similar demographics (enrollment, grade level) in their state and nationally. Survey results are available at http://www.ala.org/aasl/slcsurvey.

Essential Links: Resource Guides for School Library Program Development

AASL regularly receives questions on a variety of topics from school librarians, principals, parents, charter school organizers, library paraprofessionals, government officials, and college instructors. To help answer these questions, AASL has a set of online bibliographies that cover such issues as advocacy, assessment, collaboration, collection development, copyright, curriculum and instruction, intellectual freedom, standards and guidelines, student achievement, and technology. These bibliographies include references to books, journal articles, websites, and other media. The guides are hosted on an AASL wiki and are open to contributions from anyone who has found a helpful resource on one of the topics covered. This open format enables the whole school library community to share its knowledge and experience for the benefit of all.

Essential Links is available at http://aasl.ala.org/essentiallinks.

AASL Position Statements

AASL has published position statements on many issues critical to school library programs and their role in education. These issues include, for example, legislation, certification, intellectual freedom, staffing, reading development, and school library supervisors. These statements appear in the Issues and Advocacy section of the AASL website at http://www.ala.org/ala/aasl/positions.

APPENDIX H: Bibliography

American Association of School Librarians. 2007. "AASL Standards for the 21st-Century Learner." <http://ala.org/ala/mgrps/divs/aasl/guidelinesandstandards/learningstandards/AASL_LearningStandards.pdf> (accessed February 26, 2009).

———. 2008a. "Frequently Asked Questions: Standards and Guidelines." <www.ala.org/ala/mgrps/divs/aasl/aaslproftools/learningstandards/standardsfaq.cfm> (accessed February 23, 2009).

———. 2008b. "School Libraries Count." <www.ala.org/ala/mgrps/divs/aasl/researchandstatistics/slcsurvey/slcsurvey.cfm>. (accessed February 26, 2009).

———. 2009. *Standards for the 21st-Century Learner in Action.* Chicago: ALA.

American Library Association and Association for Educational Communications and Technology. 1998. *Information Power: Building Partnerships for Learning.* Chicago: ALA.

Braden, R. A., and J. A. Horton. 1982. Identifying the theoretical foundations of visual literacy. *Journal of Visual/Verbal Languaging* 2, 37–42.

Brafman, O., and R. A. Beckstrom. 2006. *The Starfish and the Spider: The Unstoppable Power of Leaderless Organizations.* New York: Portfolio.

Carr, J. A., ed. 2008. *Leadership for Excellence: Insights of the National School Library Media Program of the Year Award winners.* Chicago: ALA.

Friedman, T. L. 2006. *The World Is Flat: A Brief History of the Twenty-first Century.* New York: Farrar, Straus and Giroux.

Gardner, H. 1999. *Intelligence Reframed: Multiple Intelligences for the 21st Century.* New York: Basic Books.

Hackman, M. and C. Johnson. 2003. *Leadership: A Communication Perspective.* Long Grove, IL: Waveland Press, Inc.

Horrigan, J., and K. Murray. 2006. *Home Broadband Adoption in Rural America.* Washington, DC: Pew Internet & American Life Project. <www.pewinternet.org/PPF/r/176/report_display.asp> (accessed February 23, 2009).

Jenkins, H., et al. *Confronting the Challenge of Participatory Culture: Media Education for the 21st Century.* Chicago: MacArthur Foundation. <http://digitallearning.macfound.org/atf/cf%7B7E45C7E0-A3E0-4B89-AC9C E807E1B0 AE4E%7D/JENKINS_WHITE_PAPER.PDF> (accessed January 14, 2009).

Johnson, D. 1997. *The Indispensable Librarian: Surviving (and Thriving) in School Media Centers in the Information Age.* Worthington, OH: Linworth.

Kuhlthau, C., L. K. Maniotes, and A. K. Caspari. 2007. *Guided Inquiry: Learning in the 21st Century.* Westport, CT: Libraries Unlimited.

Lankford, M., ed. 2006. *Leadership and the School Librarian: Essays from Leaders in the Field.* Worthington, OH: Linworth.

Lenhart, A., M. Madden, A. R. Macgill, and A. Smith. 2007. *Teens and Social Media.* Washington, DC: Pew Internet & American Life Project. <www.pewinternet.org/PPF/r/230/report_display.asp> (accessed February 23, 2009).

Marx, G. 2006. *Sixteen Trends, Their Profound Impact on Our Future: Implications for Students, Education, Communities, Countries, and the Whole of Society.* Alexandria, VA: Educational Research Service.

McGhee, M. W., and B. A. Jansen. 2005. *The Principal's Guide to a Powerful Library Media Program.* Worthington, OH: Linworth.

McGregor, Joy. 2006. Flexible scheduling: Implementing an innovation. *School Library Media Research* 9 (April). <www.ala.org/ala/mgrps/divs/aasl/aaslpubsandjournals/slmrb/slmrcontents/volume9/flexible.cfm> (accessed February 23, 2009).

National Governors Association, the Council of Chief State School Officers, and Achieve, Inc. 2008. *Benchmarking for Success: Ensuring U.S. Students Receive a World-Class Education.* Washington, DC: NGA. <www.achieve.org/files/BenchmarkingforSuccess.pdf> (accessed February 23, 2009).

Partnership for 21st Century Skills. 2008. *Transition Brief: Policy Recommendations for Preparing Americans for the Global Skills Race.* <www.21stcenturyskills.org/documents/p21_presidential_transition_paper_nov_2008.pdf> (accessed February 23, 2009).

Partnership for 21st Century Skills. 2009. *21st Century Learning Environments.* <www.21stcenturyskills.org/documents/le_white_paper-1.pdf> (accessed February 23, 2009).

Siess, J. A., and J. Lorig, ed. 2007. *Out Front with Stephen Abram: A Guide for Information Leaders.* Chicago: ALA.

State Educational Technology Directors Association, Technology Literacy Assessment Work Group. Technology literacy. <www.nde.state. ne.us/techcen/Technology Literacy.html> (accessed December 11, 2008).

Tapscott, D., and A. D. Williams. 2006. *Wikinomics: How Mass Collaboration Changes Everything.* New York: Portfolio.

APPENDIX I:
Acknowledgements

American Association of School Librarians (AASL) gratefully acknowledges the following:

AASL Presidents

Cyndi Phillip, Grand Haven Area Public Schools, MI 2006–2007

Sara Kelly Johns, Lake Placid Middle-High School, NY 2007–2008

Ann M. Martin, Henrico County Public Schools, Richmond, VA   2008–2009

AASL Executive Director

Julie A. Walker

Project Manager/Writer

Catherine Mayer, Chicago, IL

Attendees of the Vision Summit, December 1–3, 2006:

Region 1

Connecticut Educational Media Association
David S. Bilmes

Massachusetts School Library Media Association
Valerie Diggs

Maine Association of School Librarians
Peggy Stevens-Becksvoort

New Hampshire Educational Media Association
Diane C. Beaman

New England Educational Media Association
Susan D. Ballard

Region 2

DC Association of School Librarians
Andre Maria Taylor

Delaware School Library Media Association
Jane Stewart

Maryland Educational Media Organization
Gail C. Bailey

New Jersey Association of School Librarians
LaDawna F. Harrington

New York Library Association, School Library Section
Sally A. Daniels

Pennsylvania School Librarians Association
Celeste DiCarlo Nalwasky

Region 3

Association for Indiana Media Educators
Carl A. Harvey, II

Illinois School Library Media Association
Paul K. Whitsitt

Iowa Association of School Librarians
Kristin A. Steingreaber

Minnesota Educational Media Organization
Jane Prestebak

Ohio Educational Library Media Association
Christine Findlay

Wisconsin Educational Media Association
Val Edwards

Region 4

North Carolina School Library Media Association
Jackie R. Pierson

South Carolina Association of School Librarians
Janet Drafts Boltjes

Tennessee Association of School Librarians
Diane R. Chen

Virginia Educational Media Association
Nancy V. Silcox

Region 5

Alabama Instructional Media Association
Elizabeth E. Hathcock

Georgia Library Media Association
Rosalind Lucile Dennis

Region 6

New Mexico Library Association Susan W. Bontly

Texas Association of School Librarians
Debbie Hall

Region 7

Arizona Library Association—
Teacher Librarian Division
Judi Moreillon

Hawaii Association of School Librarians
Flordeliza Linda Marks

Nevada Library Association, School/Children's
Library Section
Ellen M. Fockler

Region 8

Alaska Association of School Librarians
Robin E. Turk

Idaho Library Association, Educational
Media Division
Norma Jean Sprouffske

Washington Library Media Association
Sarah Applegate

Region 9

Colorado Association of School Librarians
Jody K. Howard

Kansas Association of School Librarians
Linda Corey

Nebraska Educational Media Association
Rebecca J. Pasco

Nebraska Library Association, School,
Children's and Young People's Section
Glenda A. Willnerd

Paul Meyer, Facilitator
Catherine Mayer, Project Manager/Writer
Cyndi Phillip, AASL President
Julie Walker, AASL Executive Director
Beverley Becker, AASL Deputy Executive Director

Representatives from the following associations were unable to attend due to weather conditions:
Arkansas Association of School Librarians
California School Library Association
Kentucky School Media Association
Michigan Association for Media in Education
Mississippi Library Association - School Section
Missouri Association of School Librarians
Oaklahoma Association of School Library Media Specialists
Oregon Educational Library Media Association
Rhode Island Educational Media Association
Vermont Educational Media Association

AASL Guidelines Editing Task Force (2007–2008):

Chair: Bonnie J. Grimble, Carmel Senior High School Library, IN

Theresa M. Fredericka, INFOhio Project, Columbus, OH

Carol A. Gordon, Rutgers University, School of Communication Information & Library Studies, New Brunswick, NJ

Elizabeth E. Hathcock, Weaver Elementary School, AL

Douglas Allan Johnson, Mankato Public Schools, MN

Cathy Rettberg, Menlo School, Atherton, CA

Joyce Kasman Valenza, Columnist, Rydal, PA

Project Manager/Writer: Catherine Mayer, Chicago, IL

AASL Board Liaison: Catherine E. Marriott, Orchard Park Central Schools, NY

AASL Staff Liaison: Beverley Becker, Deputy Executive Director

AASL Guidelines Editing Task Force (2008–2009):

Chair: Bonnie J. Grimble, Carmel Senior High School Library, IN

Theresa M. Fredericka, INFOhio Project, Columbus, OH

Carol A. Gordon, Rutgers University School of Communication Information & Library Studies, New Brunswick, NJ

Elizabeth E. Hathcock, Weaver Elementary School, AL

Cathy Rettberg, Menlo School, Atherton, CA

Project Manager/Writer: Catherine Mayer, Chicago, IL

AASL Board Liaison: Carl A. Harvey, II, North Elementary School, Noblesville, IN

AASL Staff Liaisons: Beverley Becker, Deputy Executive Director, Jonathan West, Manager, Communications

AASL Learning Standards Rewrite Task Force (2006–2007):
Co-chair: Cassandra G. Barnett, Fayetteville High School
Co-chair: Gail G. Dickinson, Old Dominion University, VA
Eugene Hainer, Colorado State Library, Denver
Melissa P. Johnston, Vickery Creek Elementary, Cumming, GA
Marcia A. Mardis, Wayne State University, Detroit, MI
Barbara K. Stripling, New York City Department of Education
AASL Board Liaison: Irene Kwidzinski, Northville Elementary School, CT
AASL Staff Liaison: Beverley Becker, Deputy Executive Director

AASL Learning Standards Indicators and Assessment Task Force (2007–2008):
Chair: Katherine Lowe, Massachusetts School Library Association
Cassandra G. Barnett, Fayetteville High School Library, AR
Colet Bartow, Montana Office of Public Instruction, Helena
Fran Glick, Baltimore County Public Schools, MD
Violet H. Harada, University of Hawaii, Library & Information Science Program, Honolulu
Melissa P. Johnston, doctoral student, College of Information, Florida State University, Tallahassee
Barbara K. Stripling, New York City Department of Education
AASL Board Liaison: Allison G. Kaplan, University of Wisconsin-Madison
AASL Staff Liaison: Jonathan West, Manager, Communications

AASL Research and Statistics Committee (2008–2009):
Chair: Marcia A. Mardis, Florida State University, College of Information Studies, Tallahassee

Douglas Achterman, University of North Texas SLIS, Denton
Linda Mary Diekman, Lake Bluff School District #65, IL
Phyllis D. Fisher, Copiague, NY
David V. Loertscher, San Jose State University, CA
Richard E.B. Lord, Belmont Preparatory High School, Bronx, NY
Anne Marie Perrault, University of South Carolina, School of Library & Information Science, Columbia
Susan G. Williamson, Albuquerque Academy, NM
Connie M. Pierce, Falling Water Elementary School Library, Hixson, TN
AASL Board Liaison: Louis Matthew Greco, Jr., Saint Johns County Schools, Saint Augustine, FL
AASL Staff Liaison: Allison Cline, Deputy Executive Director

AASL Standards and Guidelines Implementation Task Force (2007–2008):
Chair: Susan D. Ballard, Londonderry School District, NH
Angela Crockett Coxen, Roberto Clemente Public School #24, Paterson, NJ
Suzanne J. Feldberg, Otsego-Northern Catskills BOCES, Stamford, NY
Kristin Fontichiaro, Birmingham Public Schools—DMC, Beverly Hills, MI
Lucille M. Hansen, South Texas Independent School District, Biblioteca Las Americas, Mercedes
Amy E. Hughes, Northern Arizona University, Cline Library, Flagstaff
Judi Moreillon, University of Arizona, School of Information Resources & Library Science, Tucson
Frances R. Roscello, Information Literacy Consultant, Rensselaer, NY
Margaret Sullivan, Highsmith, Inc., Fort Atkinson, WI
Eugene Hainer, Colorado State Library, Denver
AASL Board Liaison: Cyndi Phillip, Grand Haven Area Public Schools, Instructional Media Services, MI
AASL Staff Liaison: Beverley Becker, Deputy Executive Director Julie Walker, Executive Director, Jonathan West, Manager, Communications

INDEX